What people a

A Living Dinosaur: On the Hunt in West Africa

Spain's book is a fascinating and hilarious romp through some of the wildest places on Earth. Strap on your seatbelt (if you're lucky enough to have one) and join the ride!
Lyle Blackburn, author of *The Beast of Boggy Creek*

Pat Spain is that rare thing: a rationalist who still embraces the possible and knows that there are more things in heaven and earth than are dreamt of. A grown-up who has lost none of the childhood wonder and curiosity that makes the world magical. A scientist who keeps an open mind and rejoices in the fact that absence of proof is not proof of absence. There is nobody I'd want to travel with more to explore the wild side of our literally extraordinary planet. Buckle up and prepare for adventures.
Harry Marshall, Chairman and Co-Founder of Icon Films

Other titles in the On the Hunt series

A Living Dinosaur: On the Hunt in West Africa

or How I Avoided Prison but was
Outsmarted by a Snail

A Living Dinosaur:
On the Hunt
in West Africa

or How I Avoided Prison but was Outsmarted by a Snail

Pat Spain

6TH
BOOKS

Winchester, UK
Washington, USA

JOHN HUNT PUBLISHING

First published by Sixth Books, 2022
Sixth Books is an imprint of John Hunt Publishing Ltd., No. 3 East St., Alresford,
Hampshire SO24 9EE, UK
office@jhpbooks.com
www.johnhuntpublishing.com
www.6th-books.com

For distributor details and how to order please visit the 'Ordering' section on our website.

Text copyright: Pat Spain 2021
Cover art: Dia Moeller

ISBN: 978 1 78904 656 4
978 1 78904 657 1 (ebook)
Library of Congress Control Number: 2021941986

A CIP catalogue record for this book is available from the British Library.

Design: Stuart Davies

UK: Printed and bound by CPI Group (UK) Ltd, Croydon, CR0 4YY
Printed in North America by CPI GPS partners

We operate a distinctive and ethical publishing philosophy in
all areas of our business, from our global network of authors to
production and worldwide distribution.

Contents

This book is for Harry and Laura Marshall. I can't imagine what my life would be like if I hadn't met them. They have always believed in, encouraged, and inspired me to be better than I ever thought I could be. The quote "never meet your heroes" has never been more wrong.

Introduction

Some of you may know me as the "(almost) King of the Jungle", "Legend Hunter", "that animal guy", "Beast Hunter" or "that guy who had cancer and catches snakes". Probably not, though. Despite having a couple dozen hours of international TV series to my name, and giving hundreds of talks and presentations, I don't really get recognized very often – unless we're talking about college kids in Guwahati, India, middle-aged men in the US, or preteen Indonesian girls. My key demographics, it turns out. I struggle to name anything those groups have in common, besides me.

I left my home in Upstate New York at 16 to live in a barn in southern Maine for a marine biology internship, and I haven't stopped exploring since. My passion for wildlife led me to create my own YouTube-based wildlife series in 2004 and has landed me spots on Animal Planet, Nat Geo, Nat Geo Wild, Travel Channel, SyFy, BBC and more. Half of the TV shows I've made have never seen the light of day, but they were all an adventure and there isn't a single one I wouldn't do again if given the chance. Besides TV, I work full time in biotech, which is its own sort of adventure – albeit one where drinking the water is generally safer. I've been bitten and stung by just about everything you can think of – from rattlesnakes and black bears to bullet ants and a rabid raccoon – and I've lost count of the number of countries I've been to.

I've had the opportunity to travel the world, interacting with some of the strangest and rarest animals, while having the honor of living with indigenous peoples in some of the most remote locations – participating in their rituals, eating traditional meals, and massively embarrassing myself while always trying to remain respectful. I am a perpetual fish out of water, even in my home state of Massachusetts. This book is part of the "On the Hunt" series, in which I get to tell some of my favorite stories from those travels.

This particular book is about my time in West Africa (Cameroon, the Democratic Republic of the Congo, and the Central African Republic) searching for the truth behind the mythical Mokele M'bembe creature with my friends making an episode of the National Geographic series *Beast Hunter*, also called *Beast Man* in the UK, "Breast Hunter" by my wife, and "Beast Master" by almost everyone who meets me for the first time and tells me they enjoyed the series.

This region of the world is amazing, and remarkably misunderstood. It felt so foreign at times and so familiar at others. I met wonderful people and found some of the animals I'd been dreaming about seeing in real life since I was a little kid. I love and respect the people, the land, and the animals, and feel privileged to have been able to experience it for myself. Please take the attempts at humor in the following pages for what they are and know that I mean no disrespect. I hope you enjoy this book. If you do, please pick up the others from this series. If you don't, I'll probably hear about why on social media. Either way, thanks for reading!

A disclaimer

My dog Daisy was the best. She loved hanging out in the backyard with my sister Sarah and me when we were playing hide-and-go-seek, catching bugs, or looking for arrowheads on the trails behind our house in Upstate NY. She would wait patiently at the base of any tree we climbed and chase away our neighbor's super scary dog (he ate a kitten once). She would also stand guard while I waited for the spider to crawl out of a crack in our chipped blue bulkhead cellar doors. It was huge, with green-metallic colored fur and red eyes, and Daisy would growl if I put my hand too close to it. She was a white poodle mix with poofy fur and perpetually muddy feet. Also, Daisy could fly, sometimes wore a cape, and would occasionally speak with a Southern drawl.

I don't have schizophrenia and Daisy was not an imaginary friend – but she also didn't really exist. Despite never owning a dog as a child, I have honest, distinct memories of Daisy. Memories that go well beyond the stories my mom used to tell my sister and me about Daisy saving us from one tragedy or another. I also have detailed memories of being terrified, like heart-racing, nearly-in-tears fear the time Cookie Monster stole our shoes while we were wading in the creek catching crayfish and pollywogs. He would only give them back when we had the Count (who smelled like toothpaste) help us negotiate how many cookies it would take for each shoe, shoelace, and sock. Daisy ran back and forth from our house bringing with her a ransom of the ever-increasing number of chocolate chip cookies that my mom had left out to cool. The monster (I think people forget he is a monster by definition) kept finding loopholes in our deals, and the tension was getting higher and higher as the water rose in the creek. Cookie Monster smelled like BO and his eyes rolled around like a crazy person's. He was unstable. In the end, Daisy came through, as she always did.

Mom would start these stories, "When you were both very small, we had a wonderful dog named Daisy," and they quickly took on a life of their own. They eventually made their way into our collective consciousness as real events, complete with details not included in the original stories which must have been added by Sarah and me. It was years later, during some holiday involving drinking (see "every holiday"), that we started reminiscing about childhood memories and one of us asked: "Did we really have a dog when we were little? I kind of feel like we did, but I also can't picture us having a dog with all of the other animals we had. Daisy, maybe?" It wasn't until then that we realized these were, in fact, fictitious stories our mom had made up to keep us entertained on rainy days in our old house. Stories that drew on real events (being terrorized by a neighbor's dog, getting stuck in a creek, finding snakes, spiders, and arrowheads, etc.), with Daisy taking the place of our mother as the heroine.

I guess what I mean by this is, all of the stories in this book are exactly how I remember them, but I honestly remember having a flying southern-belle dog and interacting with Muppets. Take that how you want. I had a great childhood.

Oh, also – All views expressed are my own and do not reflect those of National Geographic, the National Geographic Channel, Icon Films, John Hunt Publishing, or any other person or organization mentioned (or not mentioned) in this book.

Chapter 1

Too Dirty to Fly

A few months before I turned 30, I was told that the National Geographic Channel had picked up a new TV series and I had, amazingly, been chosen as the host. This series would take me all over the world to live with different groups of indigenous peoples, participate in their customs and rituals, and learn their stories and myths in the hopes of getting a more full understanding of the veracity and importance of some legendary creatures in their cultures. Despite the fact that the only international trips I'd taken before this were to Montreal's Biodome for a biology-club field trip in seventh grade, Puerto Rico for a microbiology conference, and a couple of self-funded wildlife filming expeditions to Costa Rica, I was naively confident that this series would be nothing I couldn't handle. I had a brand new passport – two actually – and I was ready to go! I had two passports because travel schedules would be so tight that I would need to have one passport with me while the other was being authorized for VISAs in our next location, then swap them out with our production team after crossing various borders and getting the requisite stamps.

It was all very confusing and supremely exciting! My parents, sister, and girlfriend had copies of all of my important documents and I'd established code words in case I was kidnapped and being held captive in some foreign location. I'd taken a leave of absence from my biotech day job and upped my life insurance to the max. Finally, I'd received maybe a dozen vaccines and had a small pharmacy of antimalarial, -bacterial, -diarrheal, -pain, -nausea, and sleep meds. I was ready for anything this world could throw at me!

The first shoot of the series would be looking for the truth behind stories of a supposed living dinosaur, Mokele M'bembe, in West Africa, and I had been warned by our series producer Barny and executive producer Harry that it would be my "trial by fire". I arrived in Cameroon after an amazing three-week trip through Europe. I had been in Geel, Belgium for that biotech day job that I was taking leave of, then met up with my then-girlfriend, now-wife Anna in London and was going to catch a train to Paris for a week-long stay in the St. Germaine neighborhood. We would then head to Bristol in England for a week of meet-and-greets with all of the production folks I'd be living and working with for the next five months, then I'd be off to West Africa! I had everything I would need for each leg of the journey in two oversized packs. One had appropriate day-job stuff – pressed button-down shirts, dress pants, nice shoes, toiletries, laptop, work papers, and other trappings of a fairly normal office job. It also contained appropriate clothing for Paris and Bristol in the spring. The other was unlike any bag I had ever packed.

It contained: three pairs of SmartWool socks (not the obvious choice for a trip to Equatorial Africa, but surprisingly comfortable, breathable, and durable; also the best at keeping ticks at bay, and they maintain excellent functionality even when wet); two pairs of antimicrobial ExOfficio boxer-briefs – stink-proof for up to 30 days; two *"Beast Hunter* uniforms" – thick camouflage cargo pants and khaki "explorer-chic" epaulette emblazoned, long sleeve, button-down shirts; one pair of well-worn leather boots; three knives/utility tools of varying sizes and functions; lots of camper-toilet paper; water purification tablets; one pack of oversized bath-wipes (designed for giving sponge baths to bedridden patients in hospitals or long-term care); lots of shot-blocks; shot-rocks; Gu; 5-hour-energy drinks and various other "performance" foods; one collapsible snake stick; one pair of collapsible snake tongs; a few snake bags; two headlamps; one multinational outlet and voltage converter; one brand-new Canon T2i; one full and one head-sized mosquito net; one silk sleep sack; a warm-weather sleeping bag; a medical kit; lots of cable ties; duct tape; Jungle Juice bug spray; 99% DEET drops; the aforementioned pharmaceuticals, and a wide-brimmed explorer hat. This shit was heavy.

Anna and I ran (me awkwardly because of the bulky bags and natural lack of grace) through beautiful King's Cross station making Harry Potter jokes and looking for the train to Paris, only to realize we were in the wrong station and had to go through King's Cross to get to St. Pancras station, where our train would be leaving from. The mix-up did nothing to diminish our excitement for our first visit to what would become one of our favorite cities. We eventually found the right station, and the gate, got into the queue (this was London – it's not a "line," it's a "queue"), and looked around. I immediately noted how this seemed like a line you'd be in when waiting to board an airplane – interesting. People were placing their coats, bags, and other personal items on a conveyor belt. Suddenly it dawned on me that one of my bags was not just perfectly suited for a few weeks in the bush, but would also come in handy if I was looking to hijack any form of public transportation or lead an extended stand-off with local authorities, complete with paramilitary-esque uniforms.

Anna is generally very patient with my stupidity. We met in 1999 at Suffolk University in Boston, Massachusetts when she was a freshman and I was a sophomore. I will never forget the first time I saw her, as it was the only time in my life I have been left literally speechless by a woman I've never spoken to. She was in a dress on her way out for the night, and I was in some dirty army pants and an old Ramones T-shirt hanging out in the cafeteria. I pretended to study the overhead menu for the entire duration she was in line and made awkward eye contact a few times, but was physically unable to speak. She was probably (rightfully) weirded out by me. She made her exit, I regained my ability to function, and I told my friends that the most attractive woman I'd ever seen had just walked out of the room.

I figured out who she was a few weeks later when it turned out that I'd be the Teaching Assistant in her intro to chem lab. I spent the next few years getting to know her – teaching a couple of her labs, assisting the teacher in others, hanging out occasionally as friends, selling her my old books. Any excuse to talk to her. I literally wrote things down to say to her the night before our labs together, then lost my nerve and just talked about the subject matter at hand, or her trip to Vietnam when she was 14 (my go-to "hey, I know a fact about you!" bullshit discussion). I sat awkwardly on my lab stool flicking my gloves against my thumb to make them "pop" and stared off in space, because I'm super cool like that. I finally got the courage to ask her out on a date at the start of my senior year. She had transferred to a different university in Boston and we were both single, and to my amazement she said yes. Our first date was at the New England Aquarium – which is the most Pat Spain thing to do, ever – and it was closed – which is actually *the* most Pat Spain thing to do, ever. We then went to a nice Italian restaurant, and when I tried being classy and asked if we should order some wine she looked really nervous, and said, "Ummmm... I better not."

To which I replied: "Oh, I just thought wine might be nice. I'm not trying to get you drunk and take advantage of you or anything." Those words actually left my mouth.

She just said: "I mean, I'm only 20..." For those of you not in the States, the drinking age here is 21, and Anna was only trying to avoid an awkward situation of not being able to produce valid ID to get a drink, so of course, I created a *much* more awkward situation. She married me. I still don't know how or why.

Anna is 5'3" and fiercer and more loyal than anyone you could meet. She's first-generation Vietnamese and grew up in Lowell, Massachusetts, former Crack Capital of America, which, if she's been drinking, she will usually tell you in the form of a shouted, "I'm from LOWELL," and an implied, "Don't fuck with me or my family" – sometimes it's not "implied" so much as "implicitly stated". She's amazing in every way – an amazing mom, super smart (destroyed me in organic and all other chem classes, and overall grade point average), funny, very kind, and as I said, *generally* patient...

"I wonder if my camping stuff will be a problem," I said, casually.

Anna – "Why would they care that you're going camping? You do have two huge bags, like an Ah-mer'can. I'd be more worried about space restrictions on the train."

"Well, I meant more my knives, matches, snake sticks, lighters – you know, *camping* stuff."

"Are you telling me you have knives? Plural? Why are you bringing weapons to Paris?"

"I'm not bringing weap – well, I guess I am, but they're for Africa."

"Seriously? Why do you always do this?" was her only response.

By this point we had reached security. I have a bad history with security. I once had a gun pulled on me by the police at a Texas bus station, I am always the "random selection" at the airport, I have been strip-searched, questioned about my clothes, shoes, articles in my baggage... Basically, I was not feeling confident.

Smiling, I put my bag on the conveyor, thinking maybe I'd get lucky. I waited, and then an alarm went off. Oh shit. Anna shook her head, slowly, reprovingly. Three very large security guards came over.

"Sir, please come with me."

"Is everything okay, officers?" I said, in my best innocent, confused-American voice.

"Do you have anything in your bag that you shouldn't?"

"I don't think so." Always a solid answer.

"You don't have any weapons?"

Almost laughing. "No! Of course not. I do have camping supplies. I'm going to Africa."

"Funny, I thought you were going to Paris, based on your ticket. You don't have any knives, then?"

"Oh, Africa is after Paris. And – knives, yes. I have three knives. For camping, after Paris, in Africa." Well, this *was* going poorly.

"*Right*, and large *hooks* of some kind, it looks like on the scan?"

"That would be my snake sticks. I like to catch snakes. You know, like Steve Irwin?"

"Hmm. Without touching your bag, could you point to where the weapons are?"

"Well, they aren't *weapons*, really. But yes." Anna was laughing by this point, likely out of anger. "Probably around here-ish?" I said, as I swirled my hands over the bag, hoping I would not be thrown in prison. They opened my bag and removed its contents. The snake sticks caused some excitement, but one of the guards was a fan of wildlife TV and recognized them for what they were. My Leatherman was then systematically made to reveal each of its blades and tools and was miraculously deemed acceptable. Same for the other utility knife. Then my locking, beltloop-attaching Gerber was produced.

"I think we have a problem."

"Can I check my bag under the train, maybe?"

"This is not a plane, sir, there is no checked baggage. Clearly we can see you're going camping – all of this [motioning to my now-unpacked bag] makes sense, but this is a big problem," the officer said as he held up my knife.

"Hmm, I really don't see why. It's a knife, for camping. It doesn't *seem* like a problem."

The knife, in many places I've been, seems perfectly normal.

No one would give it a second glance. It's a moderate four-and-a-half inch hunting-style blade, not like a Rambo knife, or something. When the guard snapped it open, locked the blade, and held it up in St. Pancras station though, it looked anything but okay.

"You didn't think *this* would be a problem?"

"Well, when you hold it up like *that*, in here, I guess it looks a little different."

"No matter how it *looks*, this is illegal in England – the blade is over four inches, and it locks in place."

"Can I... give it to you? Like, turn it over to the police?"

"Yes, I think that's best. We can just forget about this as long as you're willing to turn it over."

I was pleasantly surprised. I wasn't going to have anything rammed into any orifice! I wasn't going to be arrested, deported, detained, or even questioned! The London Police seemed very reasonable. In fact, I was thinking that I might even still make the train to Paris. I was feeling good, the tension eased, and the police seemed relaxed, making a couple jokes about wildlife shows. I decided to respectfully ask a question as I was repacking my bag. "I'm going to be traveling a lot between the US, England, and other places for the next few months. What do you recommend I do with stuff like that?" I gestured to the knife, now in a secure clear-plastic container, clearly meant to show what not to bring on the train. "What if I need it in, say, Mongolia, but have to come to England for a couple days first?"

Suddenly, all good humor evaporated. "Sir, are you telling me that you're planning on bringing illegal weapons into my country in the future?"

Anna's face goes white. She mouths, "What the fuck are you thinking?", and I get the corresponding death stare.

"Ah, no, I was just wondering. I mean, I go camping a lot and..."

"Listen, *sir*. I would suggest that you don't bring any *fucking* illegal *weapons* into *my* country *ever* again. Got it? Sound good? Sound like a *plan?*" (The last said with a mocking American accent.)

"Yes, yes, that sounds good. No, I won't do that. Thank you." We got on the train. Anna laughed, a lot, and we split a bottle of French wine. We spent the next week eating, drinking, and exploring Paris, then doing the same in Bristol back in England. It was amazing, and as our plane descended onto the runway in Cameroon, it all seemed like a long time in the past. When it landed, everyone cheered and clapped. I thought this was really nice and kind of a throwback to the early days of commercial aviation. The passenger next to me (a businessman from Cameroon) smiled, and said, "Now that you're in Africa, it's worth applauding when anything works right."

As we were deboarding, Barny advised me to have my yellow-fever vaccination certificate ready to show customs officials. It was not custom officials who greeted us, however, but a group of small men in yellow biohazard suits, with white facemasks and goggles, holding old-fashioned glass syringes of mysterious liquids. It looked like something out of *The Hot Zone*. "Best not to get jabbed by anything, bro. Make sure you hold that certificate where they can see it," was Barny's next piece of advice. One of the men, holding a needle in one hand, took my vaccination record and reviewed it, holding it very close to his face then turning away, still holding my paper. "I need that back, please," I quietly murmured at him.

He turned around, glared at me, and said, "Lots of vaccines."

"Um, yes, I'm traveling to a lot of pla –"

"Yellow fever?" he interrupted. Was he asking me if I had the disease, or if I'd been vaccinated? His needle appeared to be coming closer.

"Um, yes. No, I mean, I had the vaccine. See, this line here?"

I reached over to point, and he moved back a step, turning away from my touch as if I might be contagious. "Yellow Fever?"

he repeated more sternly. Oh God, my eyes widened in terror, my stomach clenched. What is in the needle that is now getting very close to my arm?

I blurted out, loudly, "I do not have Yellow Fever. My vaccination record is on line four of the form you are holding." He paused, his eyes seemed to smile, he glanced at the form, let the needle fall to his side, handed my paper back to me, my intestines returned to their previous function, and he waved me on.

Barny smiled and said, "The correct answer was 'Yes'. You'll get better at this." (Spoiler alert – I have never gotten better at this.)

Barny, like everyone at Icon Films, the production company, is absurdly well traveled, and the type of person you just want to be around. I describe Barny as the cool older brother everyone wishes they had. He has some of the best stories you've ever heard, and the personality to tell them. While never loud or obnoxious, he has a commanding presence that immediately draws people to him and makes you not only trust him, but makes you want to please him. This is the perfect personality for a great producer. I trusted every decision he made, no matter how crazy it seemed, and genuinely wanted to be a better presenter because of him. Barny gave me invaluable direction and tips without ever getting frustrated with my inexperience. He also has a degree in biology and looks like a blue-eyed male model. He always looks like he's just come from somewhere fascinating and is quickly on his way to another amazing place with gorgeous people and interesting food. He has an effortless "cool" about him that seems to radiate, and his tendency to look off into the middle distance, apparently lost in his own thoughts, no matter what's happening around him, only adds to the mystery that is Barny's life outside of the time you are with him. He's typically seen with mussed sandy-brown hair, a button-down shirt covering a muscular upper body, and stylish jeans. I continually questioned why I was on one side of the camera and he was on the other. The only reason I could come up with was that I was an American, and Americans like to watch other Americans.

Barny's hardest job in the series was making me look cool. At one point, he just wanted me to stand there and "look bad ass" – this came be called the "hero pose". Whenever the light looked good and the background was impressive, someone on the crew would shout "hero pose" and I would have to puff out my chest and turn my head slightly away from the camera while gazing pensively at a 30 degree angle to the horizon. The first time this was expected of me, however, Barny asked me to just, "stand how you normally would and look over Duncan's [the cameraman] shoulder." I stood normally – stooped, both backpack straps on, feet pointed at about 120 degrees, thumbs in my pockets – and gazed about four feet over Duncan's head. Barny said, "No, just stand normally, don't pose."

"This is normal. This is how I stand."

"No one stands that way. You don't *actually* wear a backpack like that and do that weird thing with your feet, right? You're just overthinking it. Right?"

"Nope, this is just me, normal. What weird thing with my feet?"

"Hmmm... okay then, let me show you how a normal person would stand/walk/gaze at the distance/eat/run/pick up fruit/ throw a rock/put on shoes/hold a goat/hold a bow and arrow, etc." Barny did not have an easy job.

Being on TV can lead to a lot of self-consciousness. Social media and YouTube comments aside, it isn't healthy to see that many photos or videos of yourself. People who don't know you are amazingly judgmental, which is completely fine. I think it's part of human nature. Anna and I often quote the Nicolas Cage film *The Weather Man* where an older couple is watching Nick do his thing on the local news station. The wife says, "I like him. He's handsome," and the husband replies, "I hate him. I hate him, and his asshole face." When people say this to the TV, no one is the wiser, but with the interwebs you can give your unsolicited opinion directly to the asshole faces of the attention-starved, self-obsessed "stars" of reality shows and further their God complexes and neuroses. Technology is awesome. Luckily for me, after a lifetime of having terrible coordination, a weird voice, and joints which constantly pop out causing me to fall over at the most inopportune times or otherwise make a fool of myself, it's impossible to embarrass or offend me, and all comments I stumble across are either ignored or laughed off. I also think I have a healthy degree of self-realization and am comfortable in the knowledge that I'm not morbidly obese, but also not a bronzed god. All of the "Fat Pat" comments are awesome because one of my best friends Adrianna to this day introduces me to people by saying, "This is Pat. He was fat when he was little." The one thing I did obsess over, to the point of actually going to a doctor, was when I noticed that in about 25% of the pictures of me, my eyes pointed in different directions. It really freaked me out. Not in a body-image kind of way, but in an "Oh my God do I have an undiagnosed brain injury" way. Turns out, most people's eyes do this to some degree, but they aren't subjected to looking at thousands of pictures of themselves from all angles, so they don't really notice it.

Outside of the airport, the first thing I noticed about Cameroon was that if you hadn't told me it was Cameroon, I wouldn't have guessed it. I don't know why, but "Africa", particularly "Equatorial West Africa" – countries like Cameroon, Congo, and the Central African Republic – held a mystical fascination for me. As naive as it sounds, I pictured them looking like... well, honestly, I don't know what I pictured them looking like. Exotic in some way, I guess. It never crossed my mind to think of these places as whole countries – with bustling cities, international airports, business hubs, and car dealerships. Yes, this is very immature and Western, but, that's what I was, and all I knew of these places was what I'd seen on wildlife documentaries. I certainly did not picture them looking like Orlando, Florida, which is basically what the outside of this airport looked like. Sure, there were military personnel with AKs and there were no "Magic Express" buses with Mickey Mouse on them, but it wasn't like I stepped out into an open-air market, a desert, or a rainforest – the most common images the wildlife shows I grew up obsessing over showed me of Africa. I stepped into an overcast misty morning parking lot of a very normal, slightly run-down airport in a humid environment. There was landscaping, hedges, mulch, well-kept grass, a rotary to drop off or pick up passengers, and chipped painted lines with signs showing the direction of transport. The weather was balmy, the air smelled of diesel, and the corners of the buildings looked a bit mossy and moldy, but it was entirely unremarkable. In fact, after nearly being injected with a mystery vaccine from a masked man, it was a little disorienting how unremarkable this all seemed.

We met our guides and I was again struck by how they would have fit in anywhere – Costa Rica, Montreal, California, or Boston. I would have hung out and chatted with them in any airport bar anywhere in the world. Ronald was around 40 and was clearly the boss. He was serious most of the time, but had a great dry sense of humor. Aaron was a bit older than Ronald and spoke significantly less English but was very enthusiastic and smiled a lot. Leopold was younger, probably in his early twenties, and spoke with a thick French accent, and Sylvester, also in his twenties, seemed to have no idea why he was there, but was ready to help nonetheless. Ronald, Aaron and Leopold were muscular and dressed primarily in soccer jerseys or button-downs, jeans or cargo pants, and flip-flops. They appeared ready for anything – jungles, a pickup game of soccer, maybe a backroom brawl, if necessary. Sylvester on the other hand looked like he belonged on the streets of LA. He was a little heavier than the others and wore fashionable T-shirts and shorts with red Crocs, and carried designer handbags. He admitted he'd never been to the forest, but was excited to see it, if a little scared. He also said that the Crocs might not be the best footwear, so he'd packed some red jellies that looked like they'd been taken off a little girl in the early nineties.

After all the "trial by fire" talk I was expecting pure chaos and nonstop action, but this seemed less chaotic than the *Nature Calls* shoots I had organized, and everyone seemed to know exactly what they were doing. Piece of cake this professional "hosting" stuff. No worries. I had spent six years as host, writer, director, producer, and financier of my own wildlife show (the aforementioned *Nature Calls*) – just hosting seemed like a no-stress deal. We jumped into a line of beat-up SUVs and trucks and caravanned into town. That first ride in Africa was exhilarating. I was imagining mambas and adders in every overgrown field and patch of forest we passed. I wanted to jump out of the car and explore them all. I took pictures of the ramshackle restaurants with lawn chairs in front and pop-up storefronts selling medicines with Chinese characters on them. Street vendors came up to our cars and tried to sell us loose pharmaceutical tablets of questionable origin, their sandwich-board advertising showing full-color drawings of a sad flaccid penis + the pills = a cartoonishly large erect phallus right from that scene in *Superbad*. There were barbershops with fading hand-painted cartoon drawings of various seventies hairstyles and mustaches, Internet kiosks where you could connect to the web using a Mac that looked like it was from the movie *War Games* or whatever device you had (the most popular being knock-off iPhones, which a couple of our guides had). We saw vendors selling VHS movies and DVDs – lots of action movies and porn – with clipart covers or pictures of the stars of the film taken from other movies they had been in. For instance, the front of the VHS for *National Treasure: Book of Secrets* had images from *Gone in Sixty Seconds* and *Face/Off*, and part of the film's description was taken from *City of Angels*. It was also labeled as a romantic comedy. (If you're keeping track – yes, that's the second Nicolas Cage reference in as many pages.)

We passed a restaurant named Big Man House that smelled delicious and seemed to be deep frying every known animal. Another place had an oversized hand-painted sign of a voluptuous caricatured woman and the words "Mama and Angry – Restaurant and Dance" which made all of us want to stop, meet Mama and Angry, and dance. We saw a large number of penis signs, many accompanied by the words "strong" or "angry" – strong I could see, but we don't usually think about angry penises. Apparently this is a desirable trait in a phallus as there was no shortage of ad space dedicated to it. One bar we stopped at on the border of the Congo and Cameroon had a half-dozen posters for "Whiskey Black", all featuring scantily clad or topless buxom women and very suggestive slogans that made all American advertising seem G-rated, even 80s Budweiser commercials.

The further we moved from the airport, the more fascinating the people were to watch. Most of them were beautiful, women and men both. In my experience, and in my opinion, there is a much larger percentage of attractive people in Cameroon than most other places on Earth — except maybe Brazil. James (our sound recordist) tells me that the best-looking people on earth are in Ethiopia, however. James was the sound recordist for every episode of *Beast Hunter* and is the most positive person I've ever met. He is five years younger than me, exceptionally handsome, blonde-haired, blue-eyed, and scruffy-bearded, incredibly bright, has been everywhere and seen everything, and is nearly always in a fantastic mood. Basically, everyone at Icon is amazing, and some of the greatest, most talented people I've ever come across, and even among this group of superhumans, James is a standout. Not only is he talented in literally all aspects of production (he directs, produces, edits, writes, is a cameraman, sound recordist, drone operator, first responder, and general tech for all equipment), but he's a remarkable guy and a great friend. He's hysterically funny – VERY inappropriate, but extremely respectful to every person he comes into contact with. He always asks for people's names, and actually listens and pays attention to whomever he is speaking with. His partner Jen is just as kind, talented, and wonderful, and they have two amazing girls who will probably never know how lucky they are to have these two as their parents.

I noticed a lot of Obama T-shirts and skirts (this was 2010 remember) – more than I had ever seen in the US, actually. Some people looked like they would fit seamlessly into any major metropolitan city, wearing Adidas trackpants, T-shirts, flip-flops or Crocs, while others were in traditional wrap dresses and carrying jugs on their heads. We saw one guy wearing a grey scally cap, a Slipknot shirt, designer black jeans, a chain wallet, and white cowboy boots walking and talking with a barefoot woman in a green and yellow kabba with a basket of mangoes on her head, with half-naked children running around them. Generally, in the States, when you say "half-naked children" you mean shirtless – not so in Cameroon, the Congo, and the Central African Republic, where pantless is the way to go. Most kids we saw went full Porky Pig – a T-shirt, maybe even a button-down, but no pants, no underwear, no diapers, and no shoes. Totally unencumbered from the waist down.

We saw vendors selling everything – sometimes at stands, sometimes just walking around with goods piled on their heads. We were told this was how to advertise. We saw a man with 19 pairs of shoes balanced on his head – I counted them – and another with a pile of meat. It was incredible, and was starting to feel like "Africa".

I do realize what an American I sound like when I say this.

Africa is a continent, and an incredibly diverse one. The people of Egypt have about as much in common with the people of Angola as they do with the people of Japan – but in my mind this was AFRICA! It was a place I had dreamt about, where every nature show host needs to go to be considered legit. A place of mystery, of open-air markets and people carrying meat on their heads, and I was THERE! I was soaking it all in, and loving it.

And then, abruptly, our car died. Apparently, I have a car demon. This diagnosis was confirmed a few months after leaving Africa, in Sumatra, but was proposed by Anna a few years before that. I have always had terrible luck with cars. I once had the steering wheel of a car I'd recently bought crumble in my hands while I was driving it. It *could* be that I buy crappy used cars and am a terrible driver, but it could also be a demon. A shaman confirmed it was the latter. To determine this, he "turned into a tiger" and used a machete to slash his own arms and various other body parts of another shaman and a female medium to show that, while in tiger form, only water would drip from the wounds he inflicted. I have no idea how being a tiger affected blood flow in the people around the tiger-man, or how that helped him diagnose my car troubles but, sure, yeah – demon, let's go with that. The exorcism of said demon was a little less dramatic than the blood/water letting. He yelled a bit, growled, shook my head back and forth in his hands – or paws, rather – mixed some herbs and liquids in a coconut shell, and produced a clear marble which appeared in said coconut full of narcotic liquid and told me the marble now contained the demon that had been the cause of all of my past car troubles – which had manifested themselves to some degree on every shoot prior to my exorcism. In Sumatra, we had popped a couple of tires, broken down in a torrential downfall, and had one car slide off the road, but this was nothing compared to the issues experienced on this first shoot in Africa.

Years before this, Anna named the demon David because far too many people call me "David" for no apparent reason – Anna's mom called me David for a year. Her dad called me Pet Store, but that's because Pat Spain sounded to him like Pet Store. But, for David, there is no explanation. I regularly get e-mails addressed to David and am called David by people on the street, and to this day have no idea why. Anyway, David is trapped in a clear marble that, much to the chagrin of Anna, is currently in a box in the closet of our guest room. She wasn't very happy about my bringing a demon into the house. I protested that, until the shaman removed him, he was living in me, and I'd been in the house with no real issues so the marble shouldn't be any different. In order to make the exorcism permanent I still need to finish the ritual myself. This will involve getting some fresh chicken blood – it's best if I kill the chicken myself I was told, but not required – and mixing it with fresh-squeezed lemon juice and water, then painting critical parts of my car with the resulting lemony-blood mixture. I have not done this yet, but am happy to have David encased in the marble. I don't need to banish him to the nether regions just yet, although Barny refuses to ride in a car with me until I do.

The day our first car died in Africa was months before my exorcism, but I mentioned the story about David to our crew as we stood around figuring out what to do next. "Oh, did I mention I have a car demon? His name is David." Our associate producer Laura laughed, but James reminded me that we were in a region of the world where witchcraft and demons were taken pretty seriously. "Better not say that too loudly, mate. I was accused of being a witch on a *River Monsters* shoot in the Congo. It almost ended very poorly." From that point on we would simply say, "David! What the shit?" anytime a vehicle broke down – which happened a lot.

Ronald told me that the general lifecycle of a car, bus, or truck purchased in America is as follows. Someone purchases a new vehicle for far too much money. They drive it for a number of years, then sell or trade it in. Another person buys the used car and likewise drives it for a few years, then sells or trades it in. At this point, it may go through one to two more cycles of this or skip it, but is eventually sent to Central or South America – where it repeats maybe two cycles of purchase and resale. At the end of this, if there is anything left worth salvaging, it makes its way to West Africa. In the Congo, the vehicle is free of pesky regulations which state how safe it must be or what parts of it must be in working condition. I did not believe this was entirely true, but I did note that the general rule seemed to be, if it runs, you can drive it. "Small government conservatives" take note – I can tell you from firsthand experience, *some* governmental control over what can and can't be on the road is a good thing. People *do* need the government to tell them when that rusted out, self-welded, fluid-leaking, flashlights for headlights piece of metallic shit needs to be taken off the road for good. Otherwise, they will drive it – and break down, and cause accidents and traffic jams, and hurt themselves and others.

Our first car broke down, smoking, in the middle of a busy intersection, on the first day. It wasn't so bad. There was a stand nearby that sold Coca-Cola (everywhere on Earth sells Coca-Cola), penis pills, and illegal cookies. The store owner proudly told us they were illegal, instructed us to hide them in a brown bag, and requested that we not tell anyone where we bought them, despite having them displayed on a shelf of his store. They were very sweet pink-strawberry-chocolate-covered shortbread and didn't seem too illicit, although James insisted their illegality made them more delicious. We hung out, debating why they might be illegal (perhaps because they're pink? Maybe they're *too* sweet and, like the proposed ban on giant sodas in NYC, are frowned on for public health reasons?) and enjoyed a little break while our guides looked at the car.

We bought many bags of "illegal biscuits" on the shoot, with the same instructions from store owners each time. Everyone but Barny and our guides thought this was hysterical. James would walk around passing them out like the host – "Illegal biscuit for you, illegal biscuit for you. Ronald – would you like an illegal biscuit? No? Okay, next time." Barny finally asked us to stop, saying the guides were very nervous about having so much "contraband" in the cars. We never did find out why they were illegal, or why the guides were so concerned about chocolate-covered cookies when they didn't mind us doing literally anything else. Want some bushmeat? Sure, no problem. Illegally cross into the Congo with no VISA? C'est la vie. Pink cookies? Out of the car!

After a lengthy diagnosis of the car by Ronald, Sylvester was sent to a store and came back with two Coke bottles filled with very sketchy-looking gasoline. I don't know much about a car's inner workings, but I can change a tire and know enough names of car parts to get by in a conversation that I might awkwardly stumble into. I feel more at ease talking about cars than any sports team, but then I do drive a Prius — so, I'm clearly not a "car guy". I'm fairly confident, however, that the fix-it techniques employed by our guides would not be recommended in any auto body shop in Boston. Aaron took one bottle of gas and filled the tank, then poured the other over various parts of the car. Interesting and unusual, but he seemed confident. Then he filled his mouth with gasoline and spat it into a few hoses, some tubing, and onto a couple gaskets. We all stared in shock, illegal biscuits falling from our open mouths. He jumped behind the wheel, started the engine, gave us a huge gasoline grin and a thumbs up, and as soon as the smoke cleared from the burning gas, we were back on the road. His breath smelled of petrol for the rest of the day, and in response to our expressions of concern, he insisted it was fine and he did it all the time.

Over the next two weeks I lost count of the number of times our vehicles broke down. We would start with a three-car caravan, then one would break down and everyone from it and all the gear would then be divided up and forced into the two remaining cars, only for one of them to die an hour or two later. Sometimes, the first car would be fixed and catch up with us by the time the second died. Other times, we would end up with everyone and all our gear piled into one car. At one point, we were sitting on each other's laps, our gear was stacked at least 10 feet in the air in the bed of a pickup truck, and Ronald was laying on his stomach, superman style, on top of all of it holding the ropes we had used to tie it down as we drove 80 MPH down dirt roads. Laura had stayed behind with one broken-down car and a couple guides. We were stopped by some police at a roadblock who started telling us how unsafe this was, until Ronald tossed them $20 from the top of the car. They waved us on smiling. We lost no less than four days of filming because of car issues.

I firmly believe the most dangerous part of this job is transportation. It's not the animals that scare me, it's the cars, and sometimes the armed militias or locals. There were problems with transportation on every shoot, but none as bad as in Africa. An old Soviet WWII bus in Mongolia smelled strongly of gasoline and the dashboard occasionally sparked, but it only broke down once. We blew a few tires in Brazil, but nothing like rural West Africa. One day, after our fourth breakdown, we were sweating on the side of the road (by "road," incidentally, I mean packed-down red clay with potholes large enough for mid-sized goats to lie in – which they did), hungry, tired, exposed to the sun, moving equipment from one car to another for the fifth time in as many hours, when I accidently let my American show. I asked Ronald if there was anywhere nearby we could "grab a bite to eat and sit down". He looked at me, with well-deserved anger in his eyes, and simply said, "This is *AFRICA*." I felt about two inches tall. Yes, yes it was Africa. And I was an ignorant, arrogant American who was quickly learning just how charmed his life was. Things here did not just "work out". "It's worth applauding when anything works right".

It was that day, just before that breakdown, that I really felt like a nature-show host for the first time. I was in the back of a pickup truck sitting on a pile of old tires with our cameraman Duncan opposite me. Duncan is a well-seasoned, award-winning cameraman. He is usually quiet, but had some incredible stories. He requested "hero pose" as we drove through a winding, bumpy, bustling outdoor market. People were selling small dried fish, some familiar and some odd-looking fruits and vegetables, and tablets and other more nefarious-looking medicinal concoctions. Everyone was shouting, people had their purchases stacked on their heads, and I could not stop grinning. Duncan kept asking for me to please look serious, but I just couldn't do it. In that moment, I realized I was in Africa, I had a crew with me, and we were in the stereotypical outdoor market. I could see it on TV – I had watched this show hundreds of times! The host was in a khaki, paramilitary-style shirt and cargo pants, looking travel-worn and pensive, there would be a voiceover telling the audience what he was thinking as he looked out at the chaotic scene unfurling outside his transport. He was riding in a beat-up red pickup truck with wolf decals all over it, and the camera would shift from the broken side-mirror to the market and settle on the host's face, blurring the background – and I was the host! I was in that pickup truck! Its name was "Jack Wolfskin" and its driver, Leopold, talked to it like a friend. "I have faith in you, Jack Wolfskin," he would say when Jack started sputtering or veering unexpectedly. At that moment, I had faith in Jack Wolfskin also, and in the production, and in life in general! It was short-lived, however. "Jack Wolfskin, you have let us down. I am very disappointed in you," said Leopold as we piled into Aaron's already overloaded 1991 SUV.

Aaron, it turned out, was the most terrifying driver on Earth. He did not talk to his car like Leopold, preferring instead to play a cassette tape with one "slow jam" repeated on both sides, over and over. James made a best guess at the lyrics: "Cold pizza, cold pizza. I have a sweater, but his is better. Pikachu, peek-ah-chu." It wasn't Aaron's horrendous taste in music that made the ride so terrifying, though, but his habit of playing leapfrog with the rest of our caravan. He would start at the end of the line, not driving for about 15-20 minutes, listening to the Cold Pizza Song in apparent meditative joy. When we asked why we weren't moving, he would smile, give the thumbs up, and say, "Yes, wait." Laura would say, "No! Please don't wait, Aaron, please drive. We are very behind schedule." The response would be the same big smile, thumbs up, and, "Yes, drive," while he sat waiting. After the required 15-20 minutes, Aaron would put the car into drive and floor it, driving like Vin Diesel in every movie Vin Diesel has ever been in. He would go over 100 MPH (his speedometer stopped at 105) down the dirt roads, barely missing goats, chickens and other cars, all while smiling and singing, "Pikachu, pik-a-chu." He would fly past the other cars in our group, get about 2-3 miles ahead of them, SLAM on the brakes making us spin out and fly forward in our seats, pull into the bushes, and wait for everyone to pass, give them a 15-20 minute head start, and do it again. After 3-4 cycles of this, we were all terrified. We begged him to please stop doing this, please slow down, please don't hit the brakes so aggressively, and all we would get in return was a smile, thumbs up, and a response of "yes" followed by some of the words we said. "Yes, fucking fast," he said after Barny asked him to "please don't drive so fucking fast." "Yes, going to die," "Yes, kill us," etc.

This driving style, while rough on us, was much harder on Aaron's 20-year-old car with over 400,000 miles on it. When noticing a strange noise or a rattle, most people would try to baby their car until they could pull over and check it out. Not Aaron. If something seemed to be going wrong, for instance flames shooting out of the dashboard AC vents – which did happen – or a loud wailing noise that sounded like a dying rabbit coming from somewhere under the hood, Aaron would simply rev the engine and turn the radio up until the car eventually died. This would force Aaron to stop, letting the others' cars pass, of course, waving them on saying, "Yes, okay, yes okay," while motioning for them to drive on. Smiling, he would open each of our doors and invite us out, congenially, pop the hood and go to work. I had already seen him sucking down straight gasoline, but that was nothing compared to his other "fixes" – my favorite was unrolling a cigarette, sucking the tobacco from inside it, mixing it in his mouth with tomato paste, car oil, and gasoline, then spitting it into the radiator. He also cleared and filled all tubing by mouth, pulling canisters of various liquids from the back of his car for the jobs. After the 4th or 5th minor breakdown one day, Barny and I decided to watch the fix. As soon as he popped the hood, Barny exclaimed, "Oh, here's your problem mate – you see the battery is being held down by a chewed old corncob."

Two days of this was enough for all of us. We explained to Ronald one night that our nerves and schedule couldn't take all of the delays. We were happy to wake up the next morning to James' announcement of, "They've hired us a fun bus!" There was a very odd-looking bus-like vehicle with a huge wooden steering wheel from a ship waiting for us. The man who drove it was very small and needed to stretch both arms fully to grab either side of the captain's wheel, so he looked like a child pretending to drive or Ernie the night-bus operator from the third *Harry Potter* movie in a navy blue headwrap and flowing white garb. The bus did not go fast, but it did get us and all of our gear to our destination that day, the river, without breaking down once or forcing us to contemplate our mortality.

The next leg of our trip involved a boat trip far up the Sangha and Kadei Rivers to a gorilla research facility deep in the Central African Republic. (Incidentally, at one point or another, every episode of *Beast Hunter* started with the word "deep". As in, "Deep in the Amazonian Rainforest," or "Deep in the Mongolian Gobi Desert." Once we realized this, there were a few last-minute rewrites of the voiceover scripts.) I'm not 100% sure what country we launched from. Part of the problem is that I'm terrible at geography and knowing where I am at any given time, and part of it is that while navigating on the rivers, we kept going back and forth between CAR and Cameroon and, it turned out later, Congo. Because of the speed of the fun bus it was nearly dusk by the time we boarded the boat, a 30+ foot dugout canoe with an outboard motor and folding chairs to sit on, which was not what I would call stable. Sylvester stated he had never been on a boat, and was a little scared as he stepped in with his jellies and Burberry bag. Aaron unfortunately, was not traveling on with us. We shook hands, told him how much we hated his driving, and he gave us all hugs and thumbs ups. The boat felt very unsteady, particularly with so many people and so much heavy and expensive equipment in it. The captain reassured us that he'd driven the route hundreds of times, and we had nothing to worry about. Then he added, "The shape of the river is changing a lot with the climate, it is deeper in parts and shallower in others. Shallow in places it has never been shallow. I do not like to travel on it at night. There are crocodiles and snakes, and in some places hippos and elephants. Okay, let's go." After that reassuring pep talk, Sylvester clutched his bag and started praying.

The start of the trip was great. Bathing villagers and fishermen waved to us, and we saw some incredible birds and got some great footage. We also saw an exceptional number of butterflies. I expected to see a lot of insects in Africa, but I didn't expect the vast majority of them to be butterflies. No exaggeration, millions of them. There were swarms near every puddle on every road we took. They flocked to the sides of some buildings, and clung to our sweaty shirts, arms, and heads whenever we stopped moving, seeming to drink our sweat, which tickled in a strangely comforting way. They swarmed the camera and mics to the extent that we were forced to stop filming because of the interference a couple times, and now they were above the river and in our boat in droves. Not that we were complaining. Of all of the insects to be mobbed by, butterflies have to be the top option.

When it started getting dark we broke out headlamps and high-powered flashlights, but the captain insisted we turn them off, saying they would ruin his night vision. We had been talking, joking, and enjoying the trip, and even Sylvester seemed to be having fun on his first boat ride, although he was clutching his life vest tightly and reminded us periodically that he couldn't swim. Interesting fact – most fishermen that I met in developing nations couldn't swim. It seems really strange, right? When you spend most your time on the water in very unstable canoes, it seems important to be able to stay alive if one of them tips over. I asked about this and, for the 84th time that trip, felt like an ass when I received the answer: "Where would we learn? The rivers are full of hippos, crocs, and snakes. We do everything we can to stay out of the water." So it wasn't a surprise that none of our guides or our captain could swim. It was a surprise though when the captain, who had himself told us how un-navigable the river had become at night, not only refused our lights but did not slow down as it got darker.

By the time it was pitch black we weren't talking at all and were in a constant state of fear. We had a few close calls with logs in the water and a couple near misses with sand bars. One log brushed against the boat while we were going top speed, and all of us realized that if we had hit it at a different angle, we would have capsized. Barny argued that we needed lights, but once again the captain refused. There was a bit of a tense stand-off before we realized we had to trust the driver if we were going to keep moving. It was his way or we would be left on the shore in the middle of the Central African Republic rainforest. About an hour passed in near-total darkness and silence, with the occasional whimper and prayer from Sylvester. I saw bats by the light of a small crescent moon, but not much else. Then, without warning, the boat stopped dead and we face-planted the floor of it. We had hit a huge sandbar, at full speed – fast enough to put nearly the entire 30 foot boat onto dry land. Ronald, executing a move straight from a Michael Bay movie, carried on with the momentum of the moving boat and hit the sand running without even stumbling. Sylvester was not as lucky, and was in a heap a few feet away having been pitched from the boat onto land. Equipment and people were scattered all over but, amazingly, were unbroken. It took us nearly an hour to find and check our gear then get it back on the boat, and calm Sylvester down enough to head back out onto the water. Despite the captain's protests, this time Barny insisted we use three headlights to illuminate the front and sides of the boat. The decision almost certainly saved our lives when, about 20 minutes later, we spotted a half-dozen huge logs directly in front of us. There is no way we would have seen them without the lights and hitting them would have been much worse than the sandbar.

The gorilla research facility, when we reached it, was rustic. The shower was a natural waterfall, and the water we drank and cooked with came from the same place. There was a sign near it with the male and female symbols on either side – if you were going to bathe you would turn the sign indicating which gender could join you – and let the hilarity ensue. Not that anyone really cared if you saw them naked. Research camps are interesting. There was really no privacy as the walls were all screens, so it wasn't unusual to see people walking around in various states of undress or changing out in the open. The accommodations were bare bones, but a nice change from the tents we'd been sleeping in. I chose the room with the most and largest spiders, my thought being that spiders might be the least dangerous bug in a country known for dengue, malaria, Loa-Loa worm, sleeping sickness, and lots of other diseases carried by insects. The folks who ran the facility were from every corner of the globe. The leader was a British woman who had lost a couple fingers in a chimp attack – the explanation she gave for why she now worked with gorillas. She was fascinating, passionate, and dedicated. She had been there for years and was raising her infant daughter at the camp. There were parasitologists, mammologists, primatologists, anthropologists, arthropologists, and lots of other ologists. There was also a large contingent of Bayaka (or Aka) people – a local Pygmy tribe who assisted in all aspects of the workers' research and general running of the camp.

They were the second tribe of Pygmies whom we had lived with and seemed very excited to meet us. They were amazing guides and had a fascinating culture which had been thoroughly integrated with the research facility. They looked at the researchers as family and took a good deal of well-warranted pride in their tracking and guiding skills. The researchers readily stated that it would be nearly impossible to keep track of the gorillas without invasive technology if it wasn't for the Bayaka. Although most of them were just shy of five feet tall, all of the Bayaka at camp were full-grown men. They had tribal tattooing and some body-modifications such as teeth that were filed to points, but wore mostly Western clothes and flip-flops. The researchers said the Bayaka loved flip-flops. They'd offered them hiking boots and other footwear, which they would accept gratefully, but then immediately discard and return to flip-flops, saying everything else threw off their balance and felt weird. According to the researchers, whenever the Bayaka wore shoes they would laugh at themselves and walk with really exaggerated high steps and off-balance shaky movements until they fell over laughing.

A parasitologist told me that the Bayaka had the largest variation and concentration of parasites of any humans she had ever studied, and was amazed that they appeared completely unaffected by them. As she said this, a very happy looking Bayaka man walked by clutching a blue plastic bag. They were amused, but happy to help, when she had requested "samples" from everyone on site. They pooped into plastic bags for her almost every day now, each time laughing at the absurdity of it, but happily and unabashedly bringing the samples to her wherever she was – eating, waking up, brushing her teeth, etc. She also requested samples from all of us – we respectfully declined. A couple days later I did contract the Loa-Loa worm parasite. Everyone on camp had it at one point or another. We were told it wasn't dangerous the first time you get it as your system naturally fights it off. Your entire body gets really itchy as the worms die, though. Your face, palms, bottoms of your feet – all super itchy. If you're exposed to it over and over again, you might see a full-grown worm crawl across your eye as you look in the mirror. During dinner on our second night, a Bayaka man walked in limping and started speaking to a small-mammal researcher (who was actually quite tall). She asked him to put his foot on the table, where we were all eating, and proceeded to perform minor surgery on a clearly infected toe. As she did, she explained, "I told them all ages ago that I'm not a medical doctor, but for some reason they don't believe me. Now, I do this stuff all the time – just minor procedures, you know, but still. They only come to me with it." The man smiled and hugged her, and, as touching as it was, our curry was far less appealing with the odor of infected foot and various human liquids lingering on the wooden table.

My spider room also happened to have a mattress, a luxury that not everyone on the crew was privy too. Normally, we would throw fingers to see who would get the nice things – a random first-class ticket on the plane, the last can of hot beer, the most stable-looking canoe, a seat in the car not being driven by Aaron, etc. Experience, title, and gender were all ignored – we were equals on every shoot. Sick crew always took priority though, and I had been feeling pretty unwell when we arrived.

Our assistant producer was Laura, or as we called her, Lady Laura of Clifton Wood. It shouldn't surprise you by now to hear me gush over the positive qualities of any member of the crew, but, here goes. She is, as seems to be a prerequisite for working at Icon, remarkable in every way. She adapted to any situation with ease – going from "one of the guys", to arguing with a porter who was ripping us off, to exhibiting the poise and grace of a royal, as her name would imply. She definitely had the most geniality on the crew, but could also be impressively raunchy and would often start a conversation with a put-on cockney accent, "Oi! Wha'we inta ta-dai, China?" She taught me about rhyming slang – somehow China = plate, which rhymes with "mate", and mate means "buddy". I never got it. She immediately felt like a long-lost relative though. Being a woman got her no special treatment from us (and she wouldn't have taken it if we'd tried), but being a very attractive young woman did get her a lot of special treatment from our guides, which we all benefited from. She's average height, in her early thirties, pale and freckly, with a devilish grin and piercing grey-blue eyes. She normally wears her long curly auburn hair pulled back in a ponytail. Just as an aside, while receiving a formal education in English slang I learned that the "T" word isn't as offensive in England as it is in the States and is pronounced to rhyme with "flat" rather than "blot". I will not, however, ever feel comfortable saying it no matter how many times it was shouted at me with various accents.

Back to Laura who insisted she would be more comfortable in a tent than any of the rooms, to which no one put up much of an argument. She set up about 20 yards away from the room Barny and I were sharing. This facility was right in the middle of the forest, so when it got dark, it got *dark*. If you had to pee in the middle of the night, it was best to keep one hand on the wall of the cabin so you would be sure to find it again. There were also very disconcerting noises at night – lots of bizarre animal sounds of hunting and things being eaten, as well as heavy feet. There is something to be said for having walls separating you from those sounds, even rotting screen walls. Laura did not have that luxury but seemed fine in the morning. She said some of the sounds seemed pretty close, and she might move closer to the cabins the next night, but insisted that she was fine in the tent, joking that she didn't want to share a room with any of us because we smelled so bad. She wasn't wrong.

I can sleep through anything – massive storms, trees falling on the house, rolling off the top bunk, being stung by wasps. It's both a gift and a curse. Yes, I can sleep anywhere, anytime, but also will not wake up if danger presents itself. It drives Anna crazy – she has a hard time sleeping anywhere other than our room. Well, I slept through some *shit* the next night in the Central African Republic.

I woke up in the morning to find Laura on the floor. "Hey, is everything okay? You all right?"

"You didn't hear it last night?"

"Hear it? No, I didn't hear anything, slept like a rock."

"Are you *JOKING*? A herd of elephants broke into camp. The alarm bells were jingling, the elephants were fighting and screaming, the whole place was shaking! How could you not have woken up?"

"Dunno, but that sounds exciting!"

"Exciting? There were *ELEPHANTS* fighting *feet* away from my tent!"

"Oh, yeah, sounds a little more scary than exciting from that perspective."

"I had to run, in the pitch bloody dark, in the direction I *guessed* the rooms were in, not knowing if I was going to get trampled by an *elephant*."

"You have a very good sense of direction."

"*ELEPHANTS!*"

Laura bunked with one of the researchers for the rest of our stay, and I can now say that I have literally slept through a rampaging herd of elephants.

After an incredible and unfortunately too short stay in the Central African Republic, we had to hit the road and head back to the airport in Cameroon. As we were packing up, we saw a smiling, polo-clad man start helping to carry equipment up to an early nineties SUV. Aaron was back, and had brought the Cold Pizza Song. Unsurprisingly, our car trouble also returned. We had the better part of a day to get to the airport, and what should have been a seven-hour trip quickly turned into a 14-hour debacle. After the 5th breakdown, Barny decided to hitch a ride to the nearest town, where he declared that he would "call a cab" – even though all of the fixers told us, "This is not a thing – you cannot 'call a cab' here." We were determined to do something, however – anything but sit on the side of the road knowing our plane was taking off without us. The Eyjafjallajökull volcano in Iceland had erupted a few days before and the resulting ash-cloud was grounding planes all over Europe. If we missed this small window, we might not make it home for another week or more. Icon had been preparing for this, and was working on an alternate travel itinerary which resembled a James Bond film in globe-hopping complexity, involving numerous border crossings, multiple boats and prop planes, trains, and rental cars, and would get us home in about six days if it all ran completely smoothly, which was incredibly unlikely.

Hitchhiking in developing countries is strongly discouraged and rarely practiced even by the most seasoned travelers, but Barny spoke the most French on the crew, had been to West Africa a number of times, and seemed anxious to get back as he had a partner and newborn son waiting for him. (Barny's wife Charlotte is also gorgeous and amazing – she is a tall, thin, blonde Argentinean woman with a very kind voice and gentle demeanor. The two of them, with their rosy-cheeked, blue-eyed, bouncing baby boy, looked like they belonged on an LL Bean catalogue cover.) Barny found a nice young family in a 1980s Honda and asked them to drive him to town. They refused to take any money, but did take some of the illegal biscuits. We lost contact with Barny for over an hour, which was honestly the scariest hour of the shoot. We unpacked all of gear from the last semi-functional car and all piled into it, leaving most of the gear and all of our luggage with Aaron and Leopold on the side of the road next to a badly smoking Jack Wolfskin (Aaron's car was miles behind us having broken beyond what tobacco, corncobs, and human saliva can remedy), and started in the direction Barny had gone. We were now a group of five sitting on each other's laps with a camera, the tapes we had filmed, and a few random bags of the most expensive equipment in a bucking, stalling, and incredibly packed SUV that we hoped could make it to wherever Barny was. We passed a few checkpoints where armed men told us, "No white man has passed here," or that, "The white man was going in that direction" – different directions from each person, of course. Just as we were getting really nervous, we found a town and saw Barny, shoeless, drinking a beer and eating some frosted cookies outside a gas station. We all hugged him and he informed us that he'd found us a ride – which was great, because the overloaded SUV was in the process of dying as we'd coasted into the gas station. Then, as if on cue, Leopold and Aaron screeched to a stop having fixed Jack Wolfskin and driven through the jungle rather than pass the checkpoints. Aaron had the familiar petrol smell on his breath. They had all of our stuff, Barny had a ride for us – it looked like we'd make the plane as long as we got back on the road soon!

The ride was with three men who agreed to drive us in

their two multicolored, refurbished, dropped low, eighties Hyundais. They spoke French and a bit of English, and seemed *very* sketched out by the entire situation. Barny, however, was at ease, continually reassuring us, "These blokes are cool! No worries. They're really chill and are fine with this." They absolutely did not seem fine with this, and kept asking, "What is happening again?" When we all hesitantly got in their cars and Barny handed them each $50, they asked, "Airport?" Barny, smiling, putting his backpack on, said, "Yeah, man, just like we talked about! The airport. Very quickly, please." The three guys seemed to think we might be kidnapping them. James, Laura, and I thought there might have been some misunderstanding between them. Barny, who might have simply snapped from the pressure of the shoot and the prospect of not getting home to his young son for an undetermined amount of time, was the only one completely confident in this plan. But we all trusted Barny. When we started pulling away, and our guy asked *us* how far it was to the airport in broken English, we thought maybe this wasn't going to end so well.

The entire day of traveling had been on packed red-clay roads. Everything we had, including the clothes we were wearing and our skin, was CAKED in red/orange dust. We tried to avoid the *Jersey Shore* comparison, but couldn't look at each other without laughing. James' teeth were blindingly white compared to his newly pumpkin-colored face. I had fallen asleep at one point and somehow managed to let only half of my face get the spray-tan treatment. Duncan's eyebrows seemed to have collected most of the dust and were triple their normal size and a deep orange, so he looked like a very serious and terrifying Oompa Loompa. No wonder these three men were unsure whether they wanted to let us in their car. They had James grinning like a serial killer, Two-Face, an Oompa Loompa, Snookie, and a barefoot, crazed-looking, extremely dirty Barny, whom they were driving an undetermined distance to an airport they had never seen, following a man whose truck was piled cartoonishly high with gear and who was talking to his vehicle and assuring it, "Jack Wolfskin, you will make it where all others have failed." We must have been the most bizarre sight they'd ever seen.

After another two hours on dirt roads, we hit the first blacktop that we'd seen in weeks and all started clapping and cheering. This convinced our new drivers we were insane. We arrived at the airport with about 45 minutes to spare. We were cheering, hugging each other, laughing, hugging Leopold, our new drivers (who seemed incredibly confused but very happy when we paid them and gave them a generous tip), even Aaron got a few hugs and high-fives. We checked all our gear and got in line with our carry-ons. We were attracting a little attention, mostly because of the way we looked and our attempts at loudly singing the Cold Pizza Song.

After about 10 minutes in line, a clearly embarrassed man from the airline walked over to us. He looked like he'd drawn the short straw, as every one of his colleagues was watching and encouraging him. "Sirs and Lady. I am so sorry to tell you this. I am ashamed."

"It's okay, man, did we miss the flight?" I said, a bit dejected.

"Sirs and Lady, no, you have made the flight on time. I am so sorry, I don't know how to tell you this."

"It's okay, just let us know what we need to do please."

"Sirs and Lady, it has been determined that you are too dirty to fly. We cannot allow you on the plane in your current state."

Silence, and then, all of us burst out laughing hysterically, laughing so hard our tears washed little rivulets down the orange on our cheeks. The man smiled.

"That is so awesome. Thank you so much. We really needed that. Oh man, that's the best. Okay, what can we do?" I asked him.

"Please take off your dirty clothes and change into something cleaner."

When we opened our bags and showed him we didn't have anything cleaner, he looked concerned. Another man came over, handed us towels to wipe our faces and hair, then asked us to strip – right there in line. We didn't have time for modesty. We did as instructed, down to our boxers. Laura was given a little more leeway and allowed to go down to a tank top and shorts. We then wiped ourselves down, turning the white towels orange, and we were all handed Cameroon soccer jerseys by Ronald's boss who had come to see us off. As we put them on, the line and all the workers applauded. We all found the cleanest pair of pants we had, tossed those on to go with our soccer jerseys, and were deemed "clean enough". Some of the highest praise I received on my hygiene during any shoot.

Customs is always a little scary – most of the places we went didn't really have clear, published rules on what could and could not leave the country as a souvenir. I picked up a few rocks in Mongolia and was told I could be arrested for "collecting a soil sample for the purposes of testing for oil or precious metals" – Riiiight. Inadvertently, we had picked up some animal and plant life in our clothes, bags, tents, etc. Some places were way more of a hard ass about this than others. Russia in particular struck me as ridiculously strict. I found that it was always best to play stupid.

The question, "Do you have anything you shouldn't?" must always be answered, "No" (in the same way, "Are you a god?" must be answered, "Yes"). If they search your bag and find that mask with the bone through the nose that *might* be a human finger, the response *could* be, "I had no idea that I couldn't take that home," but chances are they don't know if you can have it either. Best just to say, "Oh, really cool mask right? Some guy on the street in [name the largest city in the country] was selling them! He had a bunch and I think I got a good price." This shows you to be a stupid tourist – clearly there was nothing wrong with the mask that you got ripped off buying. No need to mention the tribe you were staying with, or the elder who really gave it to you after that ritual you performed with them. I did not have a mask with a human finger bone in it, but I did have a bunch of weird seeds and rocks, a huge seed-pod, a few little animals made out of carved wood, some ancient sap that the Bayaka burned as incense, and some artwork made entirely out of butterflies. I guessed at least some of that might be frowned on.

The customs official looked at me in my Cameroon soccer jersey, with my filthy, filthy hands, arms, face, and hair, and then mournfully at the carry-on I was holding in front of me, and said, "I don't want to touch you. You look disgusting, and you smell very bad. Where have you been?" I smiled and said, "In the jungle." He sneered, "I don't want to touch your bag either, at all. Do you have anything you should not have?" "Nope," I replied with what must have seemed like confidence but was really mental exhaustion, and with another look of disgust he waved me through. It was then that I realized the secret to drug smuggling. You don't need nerves of steel or secret information about an airline – all you need is to look and smell absolutely disgusting and project confidence. We boarded the plane and I half-expected it to stall. When it didn't, everyone, including our crew, clapped.

Chapter 2

"He Poops Just Like Us!" said the Pygmy Children Gathered Around Me, and Other Scatological Tales of Mystery and Intrigue

A warning, before you start in on this chapter. Things are going to get weird. While all of these stories are gauche, some of those coming up are just plain gross, and my mom will be disappointed in me for sharing them. This will be Anna's favorite chapter, however, as she finds the stories about my bathroom experiences the funniest. If you are prone to gagging, you have been warned.

"Are you wearing underwear today?" asked Barny.

Me, hesitantly: "... yes?"

"Brilliant! What kind?"

This was not the question I expected from our series producer as I enjoyed my Cameroonian breakfast of stale French bread, Nutella, instant coffee, and slightly bug-infested dry creamer. I also didn't expect him to run off without explaining why it was a good thing that I had on black boxer-briefs. Africa was my first shoot, but I had learned that questions such as the one Barny had just posed were commonplace and rarely led to a good situation for me when my answer brought a response of "Brilliant!" Barny and Harry had not been wrong with their "trial by fire" comment before this shoot.

As it turned out, that morning I had been invited by the amazing tribe we were staying with, the Baka Pygmies, to observe a hunt, and was told that I should be ready to be dressed by the Jengi (their spiritual leader – actually, the Jengi is the spirit of the forest, whom they told us this man, their spiritual leader, was possessed by. He was not the Jengi, but it was in him. For ease of storytelling, however, I will call him the Jengi, which I was told was neither completely incorrect nor disrespectful). I was really psyched for my first loincloth! Images of Attenborough wearing a penis gourd swam to mind, and I was proud to be carrying on the tradition. At the last minute, though, the kind Baka took pity on my scrawny paleness and asked me to keep my cargo pants on, under the loincloth, assuring me that, if I went without, "my legs would be torn to shreds". That sounded encouraging.

The Jengi (whom I had met the previous day and who struck me as a kind, but frail, older gentleman) was leading a group of hunters in an ancient ritual and I had been invited to join them. From a distance, the Baka look like shorter-than-average people in Adidas trackpants, T-shirts or button-downs, and flip-flops. It's not until you got up close that you noticed the intricate scarification, facial tattoos, and the fact that, when they smile, many have filed their teeth to points in order to advertise that, "We eat meat, like a cat." Today, there was no mistaking this tribe as uniquely different from any of the people I had seen in West African villages. The hunters had started the ritual without me (as I am not Baka, I could not even observe the opening), and when I was escorted to the sacred forest by the chief's father I saw a group of warriors crouched over a pile of ancient-looking weapons and wearing nothing but loincloths and body paint. The Jengi seemed to be in a trance and acknowledged me by removing my shirt and forcing me to a kneeling position. I bowed as he mixed different pigments and clay in a huge leaf he held in one hand and chanted in a language I had never heard before. He took the leaf and painted each of us with his fingers, calling forth ancient patterns that appeared to have significance, but which I was ignorant to. He then drank some of the liquid and, while chanting, spat on the weapons, on each of us, and towards the North, South, East, and West while continuing to chant and sing.

I was clearly out of my element, but tried to take it all in.

The Jengi went over to the pile of weapons and blessed the tip of each one, anointing them with the liquid mixture he was drinking. He then handed them out and, to my surprise, I was given a seven-foot elephant-killing spear. Apparently, no one just observes these excursions. I was either to be a hunter or risk insulting these kind people by staying back at camp. I awkwardly shouldered my spear and took off at a run to keep up with my diminutive and nimble companions. The Jengi had just blessed each of us and our hunt, giving us permission to enter the forest and, most importantly return alive.

The Baka moved through the forest with incredible speed and in complete silence. I could barely keep up and cursed as I got torn to shreds by thorns and stung by bees, ants, and other wee forest beasties. I was heavy-footed, breathing loudly, falling, running into things and in general not behaving like a very good hunter. I was also carrying my spear wrong, as the hunters laughingly pointed out. The Baka seemed amused by my ineptitude until it cost them a bush pig – the crew and I had been making too much noise and spooked it. About two hours in I was exhausted, sweaty, had drunk half of my three liters of water, eaten a power bar, and suffered many stings, bites, cuts, and bruises while the Baka had neither eaten nor drunk anything, appearing completely relaxed, invigorated even, and had not one sting on the lot of them. To add insult to injury, they pulled lighters and perfect boxes of cigarettes (not crushed, damp, or otherwise damaged) out of their loincloths and had a smoke break. Where did they keep those boxes? How about the lighters? It was a mystery at least as interesting as the one I was there to investigate, and proved just as elusive.

An hour later, we had lost more game because of the crew and me, and it was becoming clear we were not going to catch anything, which was fine by me. It was honestly not until one particularly close call that I even comprehended the reality of the situation I found myself in. I had been focused on trying to keep up and not make a complete fool out of myself (and failing at both), and hadn't even thought about the fact that I was on a hunt. As subsistence hunters, the Baka track, kill, and eat every animal in the forest. They can take down elephants and gorillas with spears, machetes, and axes. We had been standing still for about 10 minutes because one of them had heard an animal nearby and was trying to lure it out using a distress call. It was uncanny – the hunter was making a call that sounded *exactly* like an animal. I mean, exactly. It was indistinct from the call we got in return. I was completely enthralled in wondering how his vocal chords could produce a sound like that when I realized – holy shit, that callback is getting closer.

I was standing alongside them, crouched down in some instinctive position conjured up from a deep recess of my brain, holding a spear, ready to pounce on whatever came out of the undergrowth, when I suddenly realized the absurdity of the situation. I had never speared or squashed anything larger than a cockroach. I felt so bad about killing lab mice that I used to CO_2 them rather than the much faster and cheaper alternative of snapping their necks with a ruler. What was I going to do if an elephant came charging at me? I started contemplating the moral dilemma about potentially killing an endangered species. Sure, it's wrong to kill a forest elephant, but it's maybe more wrong to kill a gorilla. Was it more wrong to kill a gorilla? Elephants are really smart, have a social hierarchy, appear to grieve their dead, etc. Was it species-ist to think gorillas were more important because they are genetically closer to humans and look so much like us? What makes people so great? Why do we think things that behave like us are in some way more worthy of existence. Then I realized I was crouched down, holding a weapon called an "elephant spear" in a loincloth and body paint, and was having a moral crisis. It was the best example of "First World Problems" I had ever experienced. These guys were thinking, "Our families are hungry, we need to feed them," while I was thinking things like, "species-ist." "God, I am an asshole," I thought.

I was getting nauseous thinking about the entire situation. This was not something I'd considered when I'd dreamed of being a nature show host – or even that morning when I'd been excited to go on the hunt. The crew was relying on me to give them good material to film, the Baka were relying on me to help them bring food home for their families, I was trying to stay true to my own morals and imagined that somehow by making this series I could increase people's awareness of, respect for, and interest in this part of the world where a boost in conservation dollars could really mean something. That this could help protect any of the species which, ironically, I might be expected to slaughter any minute.

Luckily, I never had to find out what I would have done should an endangered animal step forward. The crew made some noise trying to get a good shot of me crouched and ready to spring, and the animal ran off without my ever even seeing what it was. I felt a strong sense of guilt immediately after the relief. I was glad I didn't have to kill anything, but profoundly sad that we didn't have any food to bring back for the people who had been so amazingly kind to us. They would not have protein that night, because of us. I knew we would share what we had and we had brought gifts for them, but still – this was not a good feeling. And it made it even worse when the hunters were super nice about it.

James and I were nearly out of water as we'd been in the oppressive heat for about four hours, and our spirits were low. We came over a ridge and found five massive snails – giant African land snails! The hunters were excited – these were a very popular food and easy to prepare. Our spirits rose a little – we would have *something* to show for our efforts. The snails seemed to have brought about a second wind, and the hunters, recognizing the weak links, asked us to hang out for a bit while they went ahead and tried to kill something. They invited Barny and I to join them, but no cameras and no sound recording. Because of the time we had lost on the road, we still needed to do quite a bit of filming, and Barny asked me to stay back and film some B-roll (me looking at trees, walking, picking things up, staring into the distance thoughtfully – basically, filler shots to put voiceover to later) and some footage of me talking to the camera telling a few facts and stories to move the episode along, while he went and joined the hunt. The hunters handed us the snails and asked us to watch them, kind of chuckling, and "make sure they don't get away". We were relegated to babysitting snails.

We filmed the B-roll pretty quick, got through all of the stories, and Barny wasn't yet back so we filmed a little more then decided to knock a couple more shots off the list. We needed one of smoke going through the trees – a kind of an ominous, dark shot to use as a cutaway. One of our guides lit a fire and put some live vegetation on it to cause a lot of smoke. It looked great, very cinematic.

I found some siafu army ants and did a little piece to camera about them. They can kill people with sheer numbers. They flow through the forest like rivers – millions of them – and if you pass out, are injured and can't move, or are too young or old to move out of their way, they can swarm over you insanely fast, climbing into your mouth and nose, filling your throat and suffocating you. These sound like old campfire stories, and it doesn't happen frequently, but there have been documented cases of it. The group of them we found was more of a trickle than a river. I decided it would be cool to show off one of their traits that benefits people. I had a whole bunch of cuts all over my body, some still bleeding, and one of the great things about siafu is that they have extremely large and powerful mandibles. If you hold one and let it bite your wound, then pop its head off, the jaws will seal the wound closed, serving as a natural stitch.

By the time the head falls off, the wound should be healed enough to stay closed on its own. I had read this, but had never attempted it for myself.

I grabbed an ant and immediately received a nasty sting, like that from a bee. Everything I had read about siafu said that they "bite readily and sting rarely". Apparently, this ant hadn't read the textbooks. After some swearing I grabbed another, and received another sting. Third time's the charm – I grabbed another ant, holding it in its middle section (not the biting or stinging ends), and brought it towards my wound while I was explaining the process to the camera. The ant did not bite, but instead wriggled free and stung my open wound. I tried another six or seven times, receiving dozens of stings and lots of bites, but never one that managed to seal the wound (they would twist their head and bite into the cut rather than on either side of it). My arm and fingers were in rough shape by this point. James and Duncan had asked me to give up, but I really wanted this to work. Finally, one ant bit and closed the wound! Success! Before I could pop its head off, though, it let go and stung me a couple times.

Oh well, time for a break. We broke out some trail mix and Duncan produced some Marmite, which he loved and I had developed a bit of a taste for, and started snacking. Within seconds we were covered in bees – killer bees, we assumed, having been raised on 80s and 90s news stories of Africanized Killer Bees. "Can they be Africanized if we're in Africa?" James pondered. We would have laughed, but were too busy getting stung and pulling bees out of our shirts, pants, and hair. Our guide was completely unaffected by them and, laughing, told us to stand near the smoldering fire as the smoke would keep them away. It worked, but unfortunately left us to stand in smoke which stung our eyes, made us cough, and was very, very hot on a day that was already over 100 degrees and humid. We ended up standing in the fire for as long as we could, then "cooling off" outside of it with the bees, then back to the fire after a few stings, and so on. This went on for about an hour before the bees gave up and moved on. By this point, I had to pee. I was a little worried that it was the first time I had to pee all day, but I had been sweating buckets and drank nearly three liters of water, so it probably wasn't a concern.

This is what I was thinking as I walked off a little in the distance and turned my back, unzipped my pants, and prepared myself. Just as I was setting my feet to assure I wouldn't fall or step on a snake or anything, I felt something, something no one should ever feel – something light but distinct landed on a recently exposed part of my body that I was confident nothing should have been touching. "Oh God, please let it be a leaf," was my thought as my eyes swept from the side to front-and center. It was not a leaf, it was a bee. A Killer Bee. All 70,000 nerve endings in that terminal location were on high alert. The new flood of sweat pouring from my body had nothing to do with the heat, it was pure "fight or flight" – in this case, though, neither option seemed valid. I was frozen, suddenly cold with fear, staring flaccidly, at this tiny insect. What should I do? Should I flick it? Should I wait for it to fly away? Blow on it? Scream for help? Scream at it? I did absolutely nothing. I now fully understood the term "paralyzed by fear". The bee was walking around, occasionally glancing up at my downturned face as if to mock me: "Oh, you think you're so tough with your smoke and rolled up papers? Who's tough now? This is *mine* now." Its stinger was bobbing as it walked, its wings occasionally buzzing a tiny breeze, its hooked feet clinging to the new land she had claimed as her own. After what felt like two hours, but was probably closer to 45 seconds, she glanced up at me and flew away. I still couldn't move. I stood completely motionless processing what had just happened. Slowly, I put myself back together, zipped up my pants without peeing (the urge was gone) and with an intense dry mouth walked back to the others. I was clearly shaken.

James asked, "Everything okay? You're all white and clammy looking." I couldn't speak, and just shook my head and sat down. Luckily, Barny and the hunters had come back while I was on my little adventure and all of the focus was on them. Unfortunately, they hadn't caught anything. Barny was pretty sure it was because of him, despite the tribe's assurances that it "just wasn't a good day to hunt". They had tracked a troop of monkeys but they never came down low enough in the trees to make a viable target for their poison-tipped arrows or spears.

After regaling us with the excitement of the hunt, Barny said, "Ah well, at least we have the snails!" and looked around. "Where are the snails, guys?" We all looked down, extremely ashamed, and mumbled something about "bees". In the excitement of the killer bee attack, we had allowed the snails to get away. Let that statement sink in a little. The snails had gotten away. An animal whose most distinguishing trait was slowness had escaped from five adults. We were absolutely impotent.

We began heading back to camp, defeated, meatless, snail-less, and exhausted. On the way back, the Baka pointed out signs of life that I wouldn't have ever distinguished from any other jungle noise and sight. "That sound is a troop of monkeys, about one mile away to the north. That track is from chimps, about six of them, who passed through maybe two hours ago. That is the track of a pig. This vine provides cool and delicious drinking water. That one [which looked just like the sweet water one] is poisonous." We drank from the good vine. It was remarkable – while I had gone through three liters of water, and James about the same, the Baka had had none up to this point. No water, no snacks, and they had gone the extra distance with Barny on the side excursion. They told us they bring nothing into the forest when they hunt (besides cigarettes) because the forest provides everything they need. They cut a good two foot chunk out of the vine for each person and held it horizontal.

They then tipped it up to their lips and motioned for me to do the same. When I did, at first nothing happened, then cool sweet water poured from it! It was like drinking from a hose. It was also the last water we would have before reaching camp two hours later. By the time we got there, James and I were in the first stages of heat exhaustion. We were red-faced, had stopped sweating about 30 minutes before, and were dizzy, stumbling, and generally acting a little drunk. The Baka on the other hand pulled out more cigarettes and began speaking to the rest of the village, probably telling them how useless we all were. They weren't wrong.

After apologizing profusely to the tribe, them laughing at us, and us giving them some of our food to make up for the kills we had lost them, we got back into the swing of village life. Life with the Baka was a fascinating mix of the bizarre, the surprisingly mundane, and the utterly unexpected. Many of the Baka were not 100% Baka. There is, unfortunately, a fair amount of racism against them, with some people going as far as to consider them subhuman, and even enslaving them. As such, they have abandoned some of their traditions in order to appear more "normal" and have married local non-pygmy tribes. Unfortunately, mixed Baka/non-Baka children more often come from prostitution or sexual assault than a true "marriage". Many Baka send their children miles away to attend school, instructing them not to tell others they are Baka. We only saw maybe a half-dozen Baka who appeared to be true, 100% Baka, and it was startling. They were just over four feet tall, wore various vegetation and grasses, and were very secretive, rarely coming into the center of the village where we stayed. Not to sound disrespectful, but I did think they were children at first. The second time I saw them, I did a double take. They absolutely had all of the features of an adult – stubbly-facial hair, greying and receding hairlines, adult musculature, defined sexual traits, etc., but were so small it was hard to believe what you were seeing. Most of the Baka we interacted with on a daily basis were a bit taller and usually wore Western-style clothes.

What I have found is that every group of people everywhere on Earth loves Adidas trackpants. It's one of the few constants in life. I mean, they are super comfortable and work in nearly any situations. From the sons of oil barons in the Middle East to pygmy tribes in the Congo, kids on the streets of Barcelona, adults in Revere, Massachusetts, and nomadic herders in Mongolia – Adidas trackpants, preferably the *Magic Mike* tearaway ones, are a staple of every wardrobe. The Baka could normally be found in trackpants, flip-flops, and T-shirts or button-downs. The clothing situation was another fascinating part of the society. There was no distinction between men's and women's clothes. Everyone slept naked, and would throw their clothes into one pile in their one-room hut. Whoever woke up first was given first pick of the clothes pile. Wake up early, and you could dress like Jermaine Jackson – as one man did, every day. He had skin-tight powder-blue denim bellbottoms with a matching vest and fat-boy hat. One morning, we saw one of the most muscular men I have ever seen wearing a little girl's bedazzled butterfly half shirt. We saw a lot of wrestling T-shirts, particularly with John Cena and lots of wild animals on them. We were told that, "The men look strong and fierce, like the leopards, and when we wear them, people know we are strong and fierce." We also saw a lot of political shirts – Ralph Nader for president (various years), Gore 2000, Kerry 2004, etc. The African politicians' shirts were intense – usually just one large black-and-white image of a very stern man on a white T-shirt. They passed them out all over their districts at voting time, and many of the shirts eventually made their way to the tribes.

Western-style clothing such as this was common, until a camera was pointed towards them. At this point the Baka would disappear and reappear wearing grass skirts or other vegetation. It was almost like they were saying, "Yeah, yeah, we know what you came here to see." I'd imagine they felt the same way Smash Mouth probably felt when they *finally* played *All Star* at their shows in 2008. "I *guess* we have to do this, right?" Seeing a guy who had just been in trackpants, flip-flops, and a Sugar Ray T-shirt suddenly emerge from a hut, looking disgruntled, in a skirt made of palm fronds and a snail-shell necklace but smoking a cigarette, was an odd sensation. We didn't want to be "That Show", so we asked them to please dress however they liked. They seemed very happy about this. The grass skirts were then reserved for ceremonies and hunting, and little kids went back to wearing Crazy Town shirts with no pants, like Crazy Town surely intended.

The Baka live in semi-nomadic communities which have been getting gradually more permanent as game becomes harder to find and logging increases in the surrounding forest. They do have a chief, but he seemed more like a greeter for guests than a ruler. He and his family shared in the hunting, fishing, gathering fruits/veggies/herbs, food preparations, and other mundane aspects of daily life. They also lived in the same size hut as everyone else. The Baka lived in combinations of permanent and temporary structures. It appeared, although I could not verify this, that the more physically distinct Baka often lived in the more nomadic, impermanent homes, while the taller, less physically apparent Baka (who were also more likely to speak French as well as Baka) lived in the more permanent huts. Perhaps this was an outward sign of a divide in the group.

The more permanent structures were Bantu-style, one-to-three room, clay-and-straw huts, with walls made of dried mud, animal dung, and straw, and the roofs thatched from raffia leaves. While they might last a few months or even a couple years with a lot of upkeep, the wet season was not kind to this type of dwelling. The ones we saw had numerous holes in the walls and the roofs needed almost daily upkeep. The temporary-style huts were called Mongolus and made entirely of bent young twigs and leaves. They were generally designed to last no more than a week and would leave barely any signs of having existed once abandoned. I was given the opportunity to sleep in one and was surprised by how waterproof it was – much better than the Bantu-style huts. I was a bit too tall for it, however, and, as my head or feet hit the sticks protruding from the walls, I would be convinced that a snake or centipede had bitten me and wake up in a panic. (This was partially from the antimalarial medication I was taking, which produced extremely vivid dreams. Certain members of the crew who will go nameless would hope for dreams of Beyoncé, Jessica Alba, and Angelina Jolie each night, as the dreams really truly would be *incredibly* vivid.)

One morning, Barny said to me, "Life really happens right in front of you in a village." He was absolutely correct, especially in the Baka village. There were no doors to close on any of the huts, so nothing could happen out of sight. People cooked, ate, talked, bathed, nursed their babies, scolded their kids, taught each other things, and went to the bathroom right in front of everyone else.

People, especially my wife, are fascinated by the bathroom situation in every country I go to. I have had some amazing bathroom experiences. Anna was fond of saying, "I'll go anywhere in the world, as long as there are at least two walls around the toilet." But my experiences have forced her to reevaluate that. There was the bathroom in a place we spent one night in the Central African Republic where the shower forcefully sprayed the entire room, cleaning it while it cleaned you. Another in Cameroon where the shower was a green garden hose sticking through a very large hole in the wall and the sink, shower, and toilet all drained to the same hole in the center of the room. When you flushed the toilet, its entire contents just emptied out its bottom and ran across the floor to the central drain. There was the restaurant with a "shared" toilet seat – one seat for five toilets. You would leave it outside the men's and women's rooms and grab it when you needed it. There were the squat toilets in India and Sumatra, the public toilets in Ulaanbaatar with the "no standing on the toilet" diagrams of a pooping man standing on the toilet with a red line through him, the same in Java to indicate "no pooping in the street", and the various forms of bidets – the worst being a *FOUL* bucket of water with a plastic cup in it that you were supposed to scoop and "clean" yourself with. This was a popular option in rural Sumatra. Other spots throughout India and Asia have what looks like a kitchen-sink hose for this purpose.

Most of the world finds toilet paper disgusting. Even the gorgeous island of Santorini in Greece has a ban on the flushing of anything other than what comes from your body. There is a little covered basket next to the toilet to dispose of all paper, if you are so inclined to abstain from the bidet. James had the best anecdote, and my absolute favorite bathroom story. I can't do it justice, but will try. Deep in the Congo is a place where the bathroom is on the second floor, and is, in reality, a bare room constructed of loosely assembled boards with a hole in the floor. What made it really unique was that it was directly above the pig pen, and every time you went in to take a shit the pigs went crazy fighting to be the one below the hole. "You couldn't help but aim at the poor little guys. You sort of felt terrible about it at first, but then you realized they really *genuinely* loved it. They *absolutely* wanted a huge mouthful of your shit dropped from two stories up. We were eating a lot of nuts that week, so maybe ours was particularly delicious? You got used to the sights and sounds of them pretty fast, but after my first time using it, I did skip the roasted pork and bacon." I believe him too, you really do get used to it very fast, all of it. It's amazing how quickly years of Americanized bathroom habits go out the window.

The commonest toilet around the world, besides "the woods", has to be "the long drop". The Baka had heard, probably from our fixers before we arrived, that Westerners were a bit odd –

we liked privacy when we did our business. They generally just went off trail a few feet to do what needed to be done. While squatting, they would still be in communication with each other and us, visually and vocally. Defecating was treated more like coughing, you would turn away to do it and would occasionally excuse yourself from the room, but it generally wouldn't end a conversation. Urinating was more like sneezing, just turn away and make sure no liquid gets on the person next to you. The first thing they showed us at camp was that they had constructed a long drop for us. It was about four feet deep, 1.5 feet in diameter, with a good sturdy log to get your footing on, and they had even chopped footholds into it to give it some rough texture. What they were most proud of, though, was that they had built five-foot walls around three sides of it. They were made out of leaves and sticks and provided a surprising amount of coverage.

I'll be honest here – despite years of camping, hiking, and traveling, I had never pooped in a hole before this trip. I was a little intimidated by it. Enough so that, the day we arrived in the village, I took a couple of anti-diarrhea meds, even though I did not have diarrhea. James was the first to christen our new toilet, and a number of the villagers waited "outside" to ask him how he enjoyed it. Laura, Duncan, and Barny all followed, each with similar experiences. James had embedded a stick in the ground next to it which served as a toilet-paper holder (the Brits all called TP "bog roll" for reasons I still don't understand) and this fascinated some of the villagers. "What do you do with this paper? Why do you need it? Doesn't it hurt?" were just some of the questions we received. The main result of James' innovation, however, was to draw attention to our bathroom habits and generate some buzz amongst the villagers, particularly the children who began gathering around the long drop to watch each time one of us went to use it.

The next morning, immediately after our coffee – which was the instant variety, with dry creamer that had bugs crawling in it – James announced, "Uh oh, gotta go, wish me luck." He returned a few minutes later, chuckling. As someone who has shat directly into porcine mouths, James isn't too shy. "The walls 'fell down' last night, and the long drop is remarkably close to a hut. As soon as I squatted, a call went out to all of the kids who then squatted next to me to get a better look. It was a little odd, but nothing was going to stop what that coffee had started. I just spoke to them. 'Hello, good morning. Nice to see you. Do you often get this close to people as they defecate? No, thank you, I'll wait to hold that chicken. No, thank you, you hang onto that stick for now, please.' They were fascinated by the wiping, also." Everyone laughed as I got more nervous. I determined that I'd put off the inevitable for another day with meds again.

After lunch, I admitted to the crew that I had never done this. "You're *JOKING* right? TV's Pat Spain has never shat in the wild?" Laura and Barny had taken to calling me "TV's Pat Spain" whenever they wanted a really good dig on something that would break the "rugged" image the series was making of me – so, essentially everything in my life not animal-related. "TV's Pat Spain can't fix our car with tomato paste and tobacco?" "TV's Pat Spain won't drink from that hot stream of elephant shit?" "TV's Pat Spain uses different face and body sunblock?" and so on. This time though, it was genuine surprise. "All right, mate, c'mere, let us show you how." Laura, Barny, and James then gave me a lesson on how best to use the long drop, as Duncan looked on and laughed. "You need to scrunch up your pants and trousers [pants being underwear in England] and make sure they don't hit the ground or get directly below the hot zone. It's a day killer if you accidently shit on them."

"Or piss on them," added Lady Laura, helpfully.

"Nice, yeah, good call. You might want to break it up your first few times, have a wee first, then drop trough for the real show, don't try the usual combo right off the bat. You want a really good squat, deep in the knees with your feet in front. Give it a shot, let's see the technique." I squatted next to James as Barny and Laura evaluated. "See how everything just seems to line up? Feel that 'back to nature' sense of correctness in that move?" asked James. My lesson concluded with thoughts on balance during wiping. "The last thing you want to do is lose your balance and fall back – you *do not* want any part of your body to come in contact with that hole or the surrounding area. It's only day two and I wouldn't touch it if I had a biohazard suit on. Maybe hold the bog-roll stick to steady yourself for the first wipe, then take it from there." This was a lot to remember, and the pressure was building, in more ways than one.

I woke up very early the next morning knowing this would be the day. As I walked by, James looked groggily out of his tent and, seeing the direction I was traveling, murmured, "Good luck, mate, you'll do fine. Remember our practice." I walked to the spot, confident I could do this. I stood over the hole, remembered the advice, and peed first, then stooped to get a good look at what I was dealing with. This immediately seemed like a bad idea when the smell hit me – a long drop in use for three days during a heatwave in Equatorial Africa does not emit an entrancing bouquet. The most disgusting one I have ever used was in Mongolia, in the Gobi Desert, the day after a nomadic festival when it had been filled by hundreds of drunken nomads. The boards were squishy with urine and felt like they might give way, a prospect so terrifying it prompted each of us to deal with the wind, exposure, and heat of simply squatting in the sand rather than braving it again (wind and used TP do not mix, as all of our boots could attest). The scent of ammonia was so overpowering that it made your eyes burn, and the heat of being partially enclosed in the Gobi Desert was overwhelming. While this, my first long drop, was not that bad, no bathroom I've ever come across has been. The Mongolia long drop reached legendary status in our crew, spawning its own stories and bets: "Getting sexually assaulted by an Orangutan is bad [true story], but it's not as bad as using that long drop in Mongolia." Or when the action slowed down: "Would you rather eat a whole durian, or eat a delicious gourmet meal in that long drop in Mongolia?"

This long drop was not as bad as the future one in Mongolia, but it was disgusting. Someone had missed the hole and, despite their best efforts, had not done a great job cleaning up, and human feces was smeared across the log. The footholds were a bit slippery from a brief rainstorm overnight, and I was a little nervous, but it was time. I was "TV's Pat Spain". I rolled my pant legs as suggested by Barny, unbuckled, gripped my cargo pants and boxers in front and positioned them in a roll on my boots as suggested by Laura, and squatted using the James technique – just as a group of children showed up to watch the show.

Everything about this suddenly seemed so very wrong. Should I stand up and come back later? If I stood up, I would basically be standing there with my pants down in the center of a group of children who were standing, sitting, and squatting way too close. Was it worse to stand there with no pants on for a second or poop in front of them? I tried shooing them away, and they laughed and mimicked my hand motions. I was sweating. Some were already leaning down to get a better look. They were shouting in French and Baka, laughing, completely unencumbered by the burning shame I was feeling. Oh God, Chris Hansen was about to walk through the bushes: "Hey, Pat, how you doing today? What are you doing here? Oh, pooping, huh? In front of a group of small children? Ever do this before? No, no, of course not. Sure, I believe you."

I had no good options. I also really had to go. The goat curry from the night before, the buggy creamer, the 5-hour energy drinks – Imodium was only so powerful. Well, I was already there, in position, so I did what I had come to do, trying to place my shirt, hands, and toilet paper in positions to block as many lines-of-sight with parts of me that shouldn't be in anyone's line of sight as I could. Almost immediately after, something flew up from the depths of the long drop's abyss and landed squarely on an exposed part of my anatomy that must have looked like a bullseye to them. My mind immediately went to the bee. It had found me! I didn't have time to think, I waved my hand back there, the kids mimicked me, and felt whatever it was take off. A butterfly flew by my face and landed on my shirt. Oh good, it wasn't a bee. Oh, gross, gross, it's on my shirt now. The kids started laughing. They stayed put, pointing, looking surprised and intrigued, asking questions that I couldn't understand, trying to high-five me, touching my arms, all while I was desperately pretending to not see them. It was awkward, pure and simple. Wiping was worse. An adult walked by, smiled and waved to me, nonplussed. After I finished, stood up and buckled my belt, the kids wandered away, satisfied that they had seen all there was to see. TV's Pat Spain had pooped in a hole, in front of a group of small children. I used some hand sanitizer that couldn't take the shame away, and walked back to our camp.

Everyone was awake, and clapped as I sat down for breakfast. "How was it? Great work! Feels good doesn't it? Very natural and all that, eh? Bet you feel better. Oh, your first long drop, we should celebrate!" I did start feeling better. It really was simply 30 years of upbringing and facts such as, "You must poop in private," that I was struggling with. Really, why was it a big deal? These were clearly only my hang-ups. The folks in the village had no issues with it. The man who walked by didn't look horrified and yell at me for doing this around a group of kids – he didn't think twice about it, in fact. I told the crew how intimidating it was with a group of kids gathered around and they all laughed and started sharing similar stories, and our guides walked over and joined in. They were amused by the whole situation and apologized that the walls had fallen down. We said it was no problem, and now that I was initiated we would have no issues with the long drop as it stood. They then told me that stories of my excretion were spreading through the village.

We were a real oddity for the kids, who had never seen a white person before. They were fascinated by our hair, our skin, our voices (which they said sounded like mosquitoes because of how nasally Westerners speak), and just about everything else regarding us. When we ate anything that they ate, they would laugh and act shocked that we would eat the same things. They had seen us eat the performance foods like shot-blocks, shot-rocks, and trail mix, and thought all of our food came from packages. We shared these foods with them and they were so excited. I caught a giant millipede and put it on my face and chased them around as they screamed, "The white man is CRAZY! He's CRAZY!" and their parents laughed. So, I don't know why it surprised me that our bathroom habits were a source of fascination for them. They were going around telling their friends and families, "I saw it! He poops just like us!"

Chapter 3

"White People Don't Eat That," or "I'm From America, and I'm Keeping My Pants"

Cameroon, Congo, and the Central African Republic are known for many amazing things: wildlife, long-distance running, soccer stars, etc. Cuisine, however, is *not* on the extensive list of wonderful accolades. In fact, it seems a little inappropriate to even discuss cuisine from Congo and the Central African Republic – places known for food and clean-water shortages. It feels wrong and very Western to *describe* "cuisine" (versus "food for survival") in these places. It is an incredibly "first-world" concept to concern ourselves with the art of food, or even how food tastes versus what benefit we get from consuming it. Real benefit, as in keeping us alive, as opposed to perceived benefit from eating antioxidant rich, organically grown, non-GMO, gluten-free pancakes. I've covered this ad nauseam in a different book, but, yeah, this will be a very self-aware and guilt-ridden look at West African cuisine and village life. I feel kind of dirty writing it already.

It would be hard to overstate how difficult it was to try to view things objectively in West Africa. I think most Westerners have a concept in their mind that, "Things are different in the Central African Republic." And they are correct, things are different in the CAR, but it's the thought that follows this concept which I believe people struggle with. Let's say you see a small child using a machete nearly as big as she is to cut weeds. Your first thought is, "Huh, things *are* different here," but is your next thought, "Oh my God, that toddler should not be using a machete! What is wrong with her parents?" or "I saw that toddler's mom hand her a machete and walk away. It must be okay"? When you see a jerry-rigged truck carrying a dozen old-growth hardwoods down a road, do you think, "Illegal logging is wrong," or "This person has to feed his family and logging is his only option"? I saw a lot of things that made me question my very Western-influenced concepts of right and wrong. Africa changed my perspective and I saw, firsthand, that there are no easy answers to some very big questions — and I will not be trying to answer them in this book. I will acknowledge that the trip made me aware of my own privilege, which I absolutely should have been aware of before I was 30 and in West Africa hosting a TV series.

When considering African Cuisine, a quote that keeps coming to mind was from one of our guides, Antoine. Antoine was an older man with short greying hair under an ever-present khaki-green fisherman hat. He had the start of deep lines appearing on his face, which was often plastered with a surface smile – it seemed that his "at rest" face was a grin, but there was sadness in his eyes, which were sunken and surrounded by very dark circles on an already very dark-skinned face. Antoine had been a hunter for much of his life and seemed to miss being in the jungle, armed with spears and giant old-fashioned safari rifles. We had spent the day traveling rough – lots of breakdowns, lots of moving luggage and gear, the hot sun beating down. We had stopped at dusk at a shady little hotel that looked like it was a missionary dorm in the recent past. The chipped paint on the walls was McDonald's red and once-bright white. We would stay the night as it was recommended that we not be on the roads after dark because of the dangers of illegal logging trucks hitting you, or outlaws doing far worse. Antoine had arranged dinner for us, and we gathered in what looked like a former dancehall or low-ceilinged meeting room to eat. It was a modest meal of a potato-like starch, two bite-size pieces of meat seasoned with unknown spices, and some rice with Maggi seasoning (which is very similar to soy sauce). He apologized for the simple nature of the food, but we all assured him it was excellent and hit the spot. In the silence, while we inhaled the food, we heard scuttering and scurrying above us on the tin ceiling. The smell of the food had apparently woken whatever lived up there, which was most likely the family of whatever the meat was we were eating according to the other guides. Antoine paused, wiped his mouth, pointed up and said, "In Africa, everything is hungry." It wasn't an ominous statement. It wasn't spoken with great gravity à la Morgan Freeman or meant to be taken with a deeper meaning. It was just a fact, and its truth was a stark reminder of where we were. The areas we were in were not barren of food, we did not see anyone who was starving, but food was not abundant. We were in and around the rainforest the entire trip, and the rainforest provides food, but not like a supermarket – it requires effort to get food from the forest. There are fruit trees, insects, small game, rats, nuts, roots, fish, and some farming along the riverbanks – while no one was starving, you didn't see any overweight people either. In some towns we would pass restaurants and bars or hotels that served modest meals, and even bakeries that made bread or the occasional sweet, but all would have signs on them indicating they were out of whatever they sold by the afternoon.

I traveled to Africa with an open mind, with a significant portion of my luggage space devoted to sustenance. I did not know what to expect regarding what we'd be eating. I knew we'd be living with two different tribes and there would be a lot of traveling. I knew we would have a team of fixers and that we would be carrying most of our food with us. The first *Nature Calls* shoot I organized was a camping trip outside Tucson, Arizona. We were going for five days and were self-funding all of it. I was going to cover meals and, naively, brought nothing but bags of power bars, which I expected would sustain us for the duration. At first, the guys thought I was joking. When they realized I was not there was a minor revolt. Eventually I cracked, and agreed to a trip to Walmart and Taco Bell to "gear-up" and get some more food. That was the first time I realized how important sustenance was to the success or failure of a shoot. It's cliched to think about stopping a scene to "break for a snack", but it completely changes the dynamic. After a bag of shot-rocks, I would be able to think more clearly, I could articulate my points better, the cameraman and I would be more in tune with each other's movements, and everyone would just be happier. Alternately, if it had been a while since we'd eaten, and the last thing we ate was stale French bread with a piece of knock-off Happy Cow cheese, I would be essentially useless and frustrated. In the Central African Republic though, there was no Taco Bell to swing by.

Each member of the crew brought their own stash of special food, but we all shared. It was a communal feel. Most of what we brought probably wouldn't be that interesting to you – candy bars, trail mix, peanut butter and the like – so I'll skip it, but know that a large amount of the food we consumed on each shoot was this type. Duncan had a taste for Marmite, which I found disgusting when I first tried it, but once I learned that it's a spread which is best enjoyed in very small doses, I grew to crave it. We also shared with our guides, fixers, and locals. Most of the fixers had worked with other crews and knew what to expect from the foods we offered them, but this was not so for many of the locals. They had some incredible reactions, particularly the kids.

Cookies caused quite a stir among a village a little ways away from where we broke down one day. About a dozen young kids were posing for the camera, teaching us how to say different animal names (I was showing them pictures in a field guide) and generally just being really funny, cute kids. We decided it was time for a break and took out some chocolate-covered cookies. The kids seemed interested, but were too polite to ask for some. We, of course, offered, asking their parents' permission first, who were just as curious. They hesitantly took the cookies, smelled them, and took a nibble. Their eyes lit up, but they continued taking only small bites. They asked their kids to share them – not one per kid, but maybe one cookie for every three kids. It was so great to see them have their first taste of chocolate, and the ensuing sugar high was very funny too. The parents watched with amusement as the kids wrestled, and jumped, and played. But we didn't just bring empty calories to the villages – we brought books, toys, crayons, and clothes to every stop we made, but the candy and cookies definitely caused the most sensation.

One guide was trying to learn English, and I would practice with him whenever we had some downtime. He was a young guy, probably 19, and wanted to visit the US – Wisconsin specifically, although he couldn't tell me why – nothing against Wisconsin, it's a great state and I've had a lot of fun there, it just isn't the first place you think of when you think of a kid from Cameroon who wants to visit the US. One day, the two of us were out on a canoe filming a reenactment and I broke out a bag of shot-rocks, which had been a big hit with the crew and our guides. He smiled really big and started motioning that he would like one, then stopped, and held up a finger to "wait" while he thought of the words in English. "Um… Give. That. To. Me?" he said with a huge smile. I smiled back. "That would work," I responded. "Yes," he replied, smiling. "Now, you're welcome," he said, as he took them from me. This was far better English than my Baka or French would have been, and I was so grateful to have the chance to spend the time with him, practicing phrases and learning local words for wildlife. I hope he made it to Wisconsin.

The reactions to the Western foods we offered were funny, but when people found out we'd be eating the same things as them they were priceless. It reminded me of Anna's family's reaction whenever I tried a traditional Vietnamese food – "You want to eat blood-clot soup? Balut? Even Anna doesn't eat balut! Are you sure? Okay, great!"

I've found that, duck embryos aside, the old saying is true, and the fastest way to connect with people is by sharing a meal. It really meant a lot to everyone when our crew of outsiders ate the same things, in the same way as the locals. In Mongolia, a huge wrestler handed me a goat-wrist that he had been gnawing on and everyone started laughing. When I dug right in and started chewing I got a pat on the back, and was told, "You eat like us now, that is good. We like you." In the Congo, we were given sandwiches of French bread and a mystery meat called "saucisson", pronounced swa-si-san. True saucisson is a French sausage with garlic – this was more in the vein of what Bourdain would call a "tube-meat". It was vaguely salami-like in texture and tasted like a mix of pate, bologna, and pepperoni. It wasn't bad, but the guides told us not many foreigners would try it, and they were happy that we tried and enjoyed it. In Brazil, a tribe killed and roasted a tarantula and offered me some as a dare. The little kids went crazy when I acted really excited and told them how much I love the taste of spider.

Another breakdown in Cameroon brought us to an odd hotel with lots of couches in the dining room. Like most places we saw, it looked a few years past its prime. The couches smelled a bit stale, the paint on the wall (stop-sign red) was chipping, and the electricity wasn't consistent. The rabbit-eared TV in the corner flickered on and off randomly, showing brief glimpses of a soccer game, along with the one light on the high ceiling and the few ceiling and freestanding fans, but, oddly, we all had full reception on our cell phones. We sat in the happy silence of texting loved ones for a few minutes before James wondered aloud how much these messages were costing. Then we put our phones away and asked about dinner.

Dinner was served by an old man with gnarled hands and missing fingers who we asked to join us. He declined, silently bowing, and returned to the kitchen smiling. He had brought out a giant Lazy Susan which contained French bread, Maggi, a small plate of mystery meat, a huge plate of white rice, and an ancient-looking wooden bowl with angry-looking chili sauce in it. It was fiery red and orange with an oil-slick on top, and the smell was enough to make your eyes water and your throat itch like you'd been maced. Antoine and Ronald's eyes lit up when they saw it. James and Laura, spice connoisseurs, were also intrigued. I watched as first Ronald, then Antoine, prepared their plates. A layer of rice, a scoop of meat, some Maggi, and a big scoop of spicy death. James followed suit, but, once he got to the peppers, Ronald placed his hand over the bowl: "No, James, white people do not eat this." James assured him that he liked spicy, and he'd be fine. "No, James, you will not be fine. You will be hurt. Your stomach will hurt, and when you use the bathroom, it will hurt. White people do *not* eat this." He was dead serious. James laughed, and then Antoine laughed, and made a "Meh, we warned you motion" with his large hands.

Ronald uncovered the bowl, and James said "just a little" as he sprinkled about a quarter of what Ronald had used onto his plate. Laura followed suit with slightly less than James. Barny said, "When you're told white people don't eat something, it's best to listen," and abstained from the peppers. "Besides, have you seen the bathrooms? This isn't the place for a self-induced ring-of-fire." Chuckling, Duncan followed Barny's lead, and then it was my turn. I like spicy, but I like spicy Mexican-American and Italian food – spicy for taste, not pain. I thought, "When else am I going to get to try this?" and decided to go for it, safely. I went with rice, meat, Maggi, lots of Maggi, and five drops of burning red oily liquid – no seeds. Ronald looked scared, Antoine looked genuinely amused. I mixed the plate together and breathed it in – it smelled spicy, way spicier than five drops of anything should smell.

I looked across the table and James was choking. His face was red, he was sputtering and coughing, his eyes were running and turning bloodshot and he was... laughing. "Wow! Shite! Wow!" Cough, cough, cough. "Oh wow that's hot.

Veryveryveryveryveryveryvery hot. But good! Oh, it's good. I *really* like it." Laugh. "I don't know *how* you eat as much of it as you do, but it's good." Laura was a little less dramatic, very composed, very "Lady Laura". She took a bite, her eyes welled, she coughed a little, and "woh" was all she could say. Barny, Antoine, and Duncan were laughing, and even Ronald seemed less apprehensive and had cracked a smile.

"I don't know why they brought this out for white people," he said. "It's almost like a dare, of course you'll try it," and he shook his head in disapproval. I decided to join in – my first bite was the spiciest food I have ever tasted. My friend makes a hot sauce from Trinidadian scorpion peppers that will melt your face off, but I've never had actual food, meant to eaten by people, that was this spicy. My eyes watered, and I coughed. My throat didn't seem to want to swallow, and my mouth was on fire. Everyone laughed even harder knowing I'd only had a few drops.

Ronald tried to cheer me up. "There is no shame in that," he said, taking a huge mouthful which glimmered with oily sauce. "We grew up with this, you grew up eating McDonald's, yes?" This made James and Barny laugh even harder, knowing that I consider myself a bit of a gastronome who tended to mock the American fast-food system. I didn't bother to correct him, and just nodded, hung my head in shame, and powered through the rest of the plate.

The chef, seeing we had cleared the plates, brought out seconds. We all complimented him and joked about the peppers. He laughed and commended us for trying it. I asked him what the meat was and his response was simple: "Meat."

"Yes, but what kind of meat?"

"Meat. This is meat." I found that, often in my travels, sometimes it was best to not think about what I was eating, pick the tiny, unusual bones out, and just enjoy it.

We did have to draw a line and resist ingesting a few things.

A shaman in Sumatra offered us a cold-tea infusion that had some narcotic properties and was mixed with local water in a coconut. We were advised to steer clear or risk spending a few days on the toilet, or possibly being too drugged out to film the rest of the day. The palm wine in the Central African Republic was notorious for killing or blinding people because it's often stored or transported in containers used to hold gasoline or motor oil. Again, we were offered it a few times and had to respectfully decline. Usually, though, we were more than willing to risk a little intestinal upset to have a new experience or get in with the locals.

We didn't always make a connection through food – sometimes it was clothing, electronics, or even politics. We were filming some B-roll of massive logging trucks in a small border town between the Central African Republic and Cameroon called Gari Gombo. I was walking past these enormous trucks with ancient trees stacked on them, some of the trunks of which must have been five or six feet in diameter. Ronald told us it looked legal so we shouldn't have a problem filming, but warned us once again not to film anyone in a uniform or any government building. The shot was a long-lens walking shot. The entire crew would be about two blocks away with the camera on a tripod, filming me as I walked past these parked trucks, just looking at them, touching the trees pensively, etc. The thought was we could put some voiceover on later about the massive amount of logging happening in the rainforests of the region, uncovering all sorts of animals and diseases like Ebola, which emerged from a forest being logged in the 1970s very close to where we were filming. Because of the distance, and the fact that our walkie-talkies had died, we communicated entirely through gestures. They could hear me, but I couldn't hear them. "Walk towards us, walk away from us, stop, look up, look down, go around the truck, do it again, walk straight, bag on one shoulder, look cool, look heroic, stop walking so goofy, smile, don't smile" –

all of these could be conveyed through a long distance game of charades. The shots often took way longer than they needed to, especially before I knew Barny well and we had established a good rapport. This shot had been one of the long ones, going on 45 minutes of walking around two trucks – I didn't know what Barny wanted and I felt like I was failing as a host (it was one of the first days of the first shoot).

A man walked by and started talking to me. I shrugged, having no idea what he was saying in his rapid French, feeling still more useless, and smiled as he reached down and grabbed my pants. "No, no, no," he said, and I jumped back.

"What? No pants?" I asked, stupidly.

"No pants, no," he said.

"I think I'll keep my pants on, thank you."

The man looked like he was in his early thirties, he was wearing a trucker hat, old grease-stained jeans, flip-flops, and a tattered looking red T-shirt with a blue collar. "No pants!" he insisted.

"You're wearing pants," I said, a little more defensively than I intended.

"You, pants, no," he replied.

I had no idea what to do, so I motioned to Barny, who raised his hands in an "I dunno" motion, then "keep walking, keep walking". Suddenly, Barny and the crew seemed very far away. I looked at the man, said, "I'm keeping my pants on," with more confidence than I felt, and walked away. He looked exasperated, and walked in the other direction, shaking his head.

We kept filming for a little while longer when another man, this one older, maybe in his forties, dressed similarly to the first man, walked up and spoke to me in French, and tried to grab my pants. I was ready for him, though, and jumped back. Barny made a "What the fuck?" gesture, then, "We need to get this shot!" I sidestepped this new pants man and kept going saying, "I don't speak French, I'm from America, and I'm keeping my pants! Jesus. What is happening?"

As I walked away, I saw a determined-looking man walking towards me, pointing sternly. This one was short, very dark skinned, in his early fifties, had a shaved head which was shiny with perspiration, blue cargo pants and a very crisp white polo shirt, and he looked angry. He walked right up to me and started berating me in rapid French. He was pointing at me, at my pants, at the crew, at the trucks. I smiled, like an idiot, then said in what I hoped was a humbled tone, "I'm sorry, I don't speak French."

"I am the boss, you can't be here." Then more angry French and pointing.

"We didn't mean to do anything wrong, I'm sorry, we're from the National Geographic Channel."

I heard the words "No!" "Can't be here," and "Jail" distinctly. "I lock you up!" said the clearly exasperated man.

"I'm so sorry, I don't speak French," was all I could reply.

"No French? Why?" he asked, angrily.

"I'm very sorry, I'm terrible at languages. I'm from America and we don't really put much emphasis on learning other languages, I wish we did. I'm really bad at them, anyway." I babbled about Anna and my struggles with Vietnamese as the man grew angrier and angrier, and his voice grew louder. I kept babbling and apologizing, convinced I would be getting thrown in jail soon and forgetting that James and Barny were hearing every word through my still live lapel mic.

"English, you speak English in America, yes?" the man said.

"Yes, English is the only language I speak, I'm sorry."

The man paused, looking closely at me and holding one of my arms.

"English, is a good language. It is the language of Barack Obama."

Oh, thank God. I love you, Obama.

"Yes! Yes it is, I voted for him. Here, look!"

I had a photo on my phone of the voting sheet when I had, in fact, voted for Barack Obama. I showed the stern-looking man, and his face softened into a huge grin. He hugged me.

"Yes! Yes! Obama is a great man! Do you know him?"

"Not personally, no, but I agree, I think he will do great things!"

"You elected him? You are the reason he is president?"

I paused, for a second, then said, "... yes! Yes I am, I elected President Obama."

I don't care if you are the biggest Trumpian republican in Alabama – at that moment, you would have also been the reason Barack Obama was president.

Suddenly, we were best friends. He put his arm around me and walked with me towards the crew. He asked if they were Americans also, and laughed when I said they wished they were, but they were all British. He laughed really hard, actually. I still think he believed President Obama and I were friends. He explained, in French to Barny and stunted English to the rest of us, that we were "busting his balls" by being there. "People see the cameras and get upset, they want to know what's going on. Why are you filming trucks? What are you trying to do? All that, you know?" It basically created a headache for him. He was the local sheriff and was supposed to know what was going on at all times in his town. He didn't know about us. "You should have come to see me as soon as you stopped. I should be your first stop. You should meet me, explain what you want to do, and we can have a drink and talk."

"We didn't know that, I'm sorry," Barny said.

"No, no, your American friend explained. National Geographic Channel. It's okay, you should know better now though. Ball-ache for me, you know? Sorry, miss," he looked at Laura.

"We certainly don't want to cause you a ball-ache," she said with a grin.

"Okay, so did you get everything you need? Are you leaving?

Did you pay a filming fee?"

A small fee was immediately provided.

"Excellent, yes, this all seems to be in order. Ball-ache over! Thank you. Obama!" He turned to leave.

"Just out of curiosity, why were people grabbing my pants?" I asked.

"Oh! Yes, I forgot to tell you – they are illegal."

"Pants?"

"Ha, ha, ha, ha," he had a great, deep, belly laugh. "No! Ha, ha, ha. This pattern [camouflage]. It means you are part of an army or a militia. It is illegal to wear this pattern here. You aren't in the army though, right?"

My "uniform" had gone through a rigorous vetting process. Over a dozen different full outfits – pants, shirts, hats, shoes, backpacks, etc. had been purchased and I then staged a photo-shoot in my apartment with Anna as the photographer and submitted images of dozens of combinations of the aforementioned outfits – as well as hair and beard styles. These photos were then viewed at production meetings and the top three choices of all of the above were submitted to the network, who ultimately decided on "the look". None of those people approving this outfit considered whether the clothes were actually illegal in any of the countries I'd be heading to. And really, why would they? And yet, here we were.

"No, no, I'm not in the Army, but these are the only pants I have."

"Maybe it would be best to stay out of any town. Stick to the jungles, and you should be okay."

And, with a hug and another shout of, "O-ba-ma!" he was gone.

After he left and as we were packing up and jumping back in the car, the crew reminded me that they heard the entire exchange. "I'm keeping my pants!" was all James could say, and laugh. "I'm from America, and I'm keeping my pants!"

Chapter 4

I Went to the Danger Zone, Danger Zone

There is a small stretch of water which inspires so much fear in the local population that they almost unilaterally avoid it. It is so deadly that it is unironically called "The Danger Zone". At least this is what certain Mokele M'bembe (MM for short) experts would have you believe. And I went there. I went to the Danger Zone. Danger Zone. Baby. Right. In. To. The. Danger Zone. Danger Zone.

Since first hearing about this place from a local contact named Arnold while researching for the episode, I wanted to go to the Danger Zone. Right into the Danger Zone. (I'm not going to stop doing that joke, as a heads up.) It's a stretch of river bordering Cameroon and Congo that is a supposed hotbed of MM activity (MM being a living dinosaur). But MM is not the only danger that's supposed to be there. Oh no — there are also dangerously fast rapids, rocks jutting out of the water waiting to smash sampans, crocodiles, and monitor lizards, but no hippos. The lack of hippos is supposedly evidence of the presence of MM, who apparently hates Hippos. I mean, don't get me wrong — hippos are kind of jerks. They pee backward, fling their poop everywhere with a helicopter blade-like tail, sweat pinkish bloody goo, attack people and other animals, and generally take over any place they damn well want to. But it seems like a stretch to say, "There are no hippos, so there must be a dinosaur here," when we know that human conflict is the main cause of hippos disappearing from different areas. It would be like my saying, "There are no sheep in Boston's Back Bay. We know there *used* to be sheep there. We also 'know' that dragons eat sheep. So, logically, there must be dragons in the Back Bay." Logic for the win. Try to argue with that.

Anyway, when gearing up for this trip we decided we'd rent a sonar device to see what was under the deep waters of the Forbidden/Danger Zone. We also reserved a powerful motorized boat to fight the rapids and prepaid for the expected gasoline usage. I've worked with crocs and monitors before, but brushed up on my knowledge, even preparing a noose-like rope trap to grab one when the opportunity presented itself. We loaded Kenny Loggins on our iPhones and thought we were ready for anything. We were wrong.

Trouble first hit before we even got on the water. Our boat was not there, and the owner refused to bring it until we prepaid for gas. We had the paperwork to show we had done this when we were back in England. We were told we had paid the wrong person – our captain needed cash, now. By this point on our trip to Cameroon we had realized that this kind of minor rip-off was all too common, and was just how things were done. The goal was to not get ripped off too badly. It wasn't a matter of a lot of money, probably $100 US, but it was "the principle", said a very red-faced Laura, as in, "if he knows he can rip us off, everything from this point on will triple in price". This was a known fact, and our fixers re-enforced it daily. They often stepped in as the intermediary, arguing on our behalf, sometimes for over an hour, about a $5 overcharge. Those charges could up faster than you'd imagine though, and if you paid one without a fight, dozens more would be applied.

Every 10 miles or so in the borderlands of the Central African Republic, the Congo, and Cameroon there is a checkpoint. Some seem more official than others. They range from a small government-chique, single-room booth, decked out with national colors and soccer-team jerseys, adjacent to a long, once-electronic, now-manual white-and-red board across the road at chest height like you'd see entering or exiting a parking garage, to a straight-up tree across the road with a group of very sweaty men in homemade uniforms gathered on either side of it, ready to open the passage – for a fee.

These started as terrifying, but quickly became more of a nuisance. We were told these checkpoints have a local rate, a visitor rate, and then our rate – the government "official" manning it would take one quick look at the passengers and the amount of gear, and the price would exponentially grow. It was still not much, usually around $7. Sometimes a dubious reason was given to explain why we had to pay, other times the official would just gleefully say, "Americans! Yes! I will take my money, thankyouthankyouthankyou!" accompanied on one occasion by a little dance. It's unfair to categorize these as "bribes". Yes, if we didn't pay them, there would be "trouble", as we were often told – "I could hold you here for 10 days to check and make sure all of your papers are real, or you can pay $10, US, and the check will go much faster" – but "bribe" still seems wrong. In reality, these low-level government officials were often not paid by any government, despite being employed by them — sometimes elected, sometimes appointed — and providing a security service to the local community. They were usually provided with a uniform, though sometimes they made their own, and an (often broken) AK47, and most, if not all, of their pay came from these "fees". "It's just the way it works," our guide Ronald explained. "Just go with it and let me do all the talking." And we did, at every stop.

There was one that got a little hairy. There was a very large tree clearly cut down to completely block the road, and no apparent way around it. It was also too large for the normal sweaty men to simply roll to the side, and there was no booth in sight. Sensing that something wasn't right, our driver quickly started to turn the car around without a word, but before he could 15-20 very muscular, sweaty, shirtless men carrying machetes surrounded us. Our fixer Ronald quickly said under his breath, "Let me talk to them, do not look at them. Look at your feet and don't say a word, even if they talk to you." The mood in the car immediately changed. We had gone from a lively conversation about what our "last meal" would be to a thick, uncomfortable silence. One of the men approached the window. Our driver, normally the boldest and most defiant at checkpoints, arguing loudly with the officials and making faces at them to make us laugh, was cowed, with his head straight down, chin on chest. This was bad.

Ronald quickly spoke up. "Hello, it's unfortunate a tree fell across the road near your village. It must be frustrating to have people stopping here."

"We can help you leave this place, but it will be expensive," said one of the men.

"We are happy to have your help, thank you. What should we do?"

"First you pay."

"That seems fair, we are happy to pay for your help. How much do we pay you? I can offer you $3, US."

"I said this would be expensive." The men with machetes took a step closer, and one reached in the car's open window to unlock the door.

Ronald moved his hands in a "please stop" motion, and the man reaching into the car froze. "That is not necessary, I am in charge here, I am leading these people. I have all of the appropriate paperwork if you need to see it."

"We do not need to see paperwork, we need to see money."

"Very well, will $10 US dollars get us the help we need to leave here?" Normally, Ronald would never jump from 3 to 10, but this seemed to be going downhill, and $10 at least looked like a number that was within negotiating range.

"Please give me the $10."

Ronald counted it out in all $1s, looking distraught.

"This is not enough."

Ronald added $3, looking still more glum.

"This is still not enough."

"Please tell me how much."

"It will be a lot. It will be hard for you to pay it."

"Please tell me how much, we will try to pay it."

"It will be [pause for dramatic effect] 20 US dollars."

"Can we please give you $14?" Ronald produced the extra $1.

"20. US."

Though we couldn't follow the conversation at the time (Ronald filled us in later on what was said), we all understood the numbers, and were aching to say: "Give him the fucking $20 and let's get out of here!" But we did as we were told and kept our heads down as this went on for another agonizing five minutes.

Ronald, having counted out $14 US, looked to borrow money from the driver, asking for "1,200 Central African Francs," which was about $2.

"No, more," said the man with the machete, and reached into the car again.

Ronald flipped open the glove compartment and pulled out more money. "$14 US and 3,000 Francs?" he said.

The man turned to converse with the others. "Yes, we will help you," he then said to us.

"Thank you," said Ronald, stony-faced.

The men stepped back from the car, moved to the side of the road and removed some foliage that was hiding a path cut through the forest around the tree. They motioned for us to drive towards them. It took about 10 minutes with the men pushing the car, laying boards to get over bumps, etc., before we were back on the road. Ronald and machete shook hands, and machete smiled and wished us well.

A few minutes later, when we all regained the powers of speech, we asked Ronald what had just happened and why he didn't give the man $20. Ronald had a roll of about $2,000 in cash stashed in his boots. "If I had given him $20, the fee might have jumped to $5,000. These are the games you have to play here."

Compared to 20 machete-wielding men, the tiny, angry, tantrum-throwing boat captain was nothing. But it was the principle. We refused the boat for the first day, deciding to call his bluff. We did a lot of filming in the village, and at the end of the day the captain came back with his proverbial tail between his legs and agreed to a smaller gasoline fee, but insisted that any unused gas at the end was his to keep. We agreed and went to sleep knowing we would enter the danger zone the next day.

Spirits were high as we packed up our gear, the sonar, and other pieces of kit and started towards the water early in the morning, just after sun up. Much Kenny Loggins was sung, interspersed with verses of *I'm On a Boat!* by The Lonely Island. Laura rolled her eyes at our immaturity until we played her The Lonely Island video and she got onboard with it (pun intended) and joined in, randomly shouting catch phrases from the song.

We walked out of the jungle into a clearing and heard running water. The sun was high and the temperature well on its way into the triple digits already. We were sweaty from lugging all the gear we would need on the boat but in good spirits when we first laid eyes on the infamous stretch of river. "There it is!" our excited guide said. "The Danger Zone!" It looked remarkably indistinct from every other stretch of river we had been on.

Looks *can* be deceiving, but not with the Danger Zone. After nearly nine hours in the baking sun of a 112 degree day, I can tell you that the Danger Zone is not so named because of a dinosaur, or any real danger. We asked our guide Arnold how deep it was, and he estimated a very generous three meters (10 feet), which would more than double in the rainy season.

The first thing we did was take a trip up and down the river, covering the entire zone.

Barny: "I can see the bottom in nearly every spot. This can't be more than four or five feet deep, Arnold. There are a bunch of rocks around the bends, and if the water was higher I would guess this would be sort of dangerous to navigate. But right now, it's beautiful."

Laura: "Yeah, the banks on the shore here look almost inviting."

Pat: "Those are perfect basking spots for crocs. I've seen a few slides from them or monitors leading into the water. Also, great places for big animals to come out of the jungle and get a drink, so maybe we can still get some great footage."

Arnold: "People are very afraid to come here. It is forbidden because of MM."

Barny, who is fluent in French, turned to the Baka on our boat: "Do you fish here?"

Baka: "Yes, all the time. There is very good fishing around here, especially when the water is deeper. When the water is shallow like this and you can see everything in it, our children can come to the shore to enjoy it."

Again, to the right tune – Danger Zone, Danger Zone. Pygmy children play, and bathe, in the, Danger Zone, Danger Zone.

We also heard the distinct sounds of illegal logging not too far away – a sign that ships carrying the logs traveled these waterways at least somewhat regularly.

When we got to the shore we saw what we expected – a number of animal prints, large and small, and some distinctly flip-flop-shaped prints of different sizes. We set up a bunch of camera traps at different places that looked promising for animals – near where we saw prints and found signs of potential croc slides, near easy access routes to the forest, etc., while also traveling further up river. After a while we found an island that Arnold had told us about – warned us about, might be more accurate. We were surprised to see that the current picked up a little around it and the water actually became deep enough so the riverbed wasn't visible. When we mentioned this to Arnold he perked right up, and started telling us about how many sightings there were near this island, how dangerous it was to be there, and why we should think about abandoning the search and heading back. The dire warning was somewhat diminished by the giant grin on his face from finally finding something we might be able to investigate, and the prospect that maybe he could get us to abandon the search before it really started and proved everything he had said about how dangerous this area was to be a lie. We set up two camera traps after a quick survey of the island and then thought we'd try our luck with the sonar, to the growing dismay of Arnold who resorted to saying that perhaps we would like to turn back as the day was getting so hot.

It *was* hot, brutally so. My friend and cohort in adventuring Dom has told me that a few things do not translate to video or paper – rain, heat, and cold. I'll try my best here, though, because it was disgustingly hot. I was sweating to the point where it looked like I'd gone swimming and was reapplying sunblock every 15 minutes. The poor Brits, a pale people, were fairing worse and had already begun to develop a lobster-hued complexion. Up until this point, the sonar had only been tested in Bristol, England, and when we turned it on we realized its inner workings were enjoying the heat about as much as us. James came to the rescue and tinkered with it for about 20 minutes while the rest of us dripped.

James realized that the only way to make it work was to keep it out of direct sunlight, which meant throwing a tarp over the poor operator and reader and essentially creating a sweatbox while they stared into a six-inch screen, trying to distinguish logs and rocks from crocs and dinosaurs. Everyone was suffering in the heat and sun, but James and I alternated from cooking under the tarp, to popping into direct sun, and back under the tarp. It was the most uncomfortable I had been in my life up until that point. My levels of discomfort would increase on each shoot, like Peter in *Office Space* when he says: "Ever since I started working, every single day of my life has been worse than the day before it. So that means that every single day that you see me is the worst day of my life." Mine were not bad days at all, just exceptionally uncomfortable progressing from the Danger Zone.

We had yet to put the sonar in the water, but a few members of the team were so uncomfortable that they would have cried if their tears wouldn't have immediately turned into little cartoonish poofs of smoke. Everyone had a turn under the tarp trying to fiddle with the controls and there was debate over which was worse – the baking, burning, drying sun, or the obscene sweatbox under the tarp. The heat under that thing was beyond oppressive – it was heavy. It was like being swaddled against your will in woolen blankets and then having a group of unbathed mastiffs lay on top of you. The sonar was on the end of a nine-foot pole. We placed it in the water, and it hit the bottom almost immediately, causing the screen to go black.

"You must be joking! It's not even five feet deep," said Laura, as James popped back under the tarp with me and Barny, and starting fiddling with more controls.

"The water is very low in the Danger Zone right now," said Arnold.

"I've had enough of this Danger Zone shit," was all Barny could say as sweat dripped off of his red face.

After about two hours and nearly four liters of water each, we had the sonar affixed loosely to the boat around two and a half feet beneath the surface. James and I were under the tarp, huddled like a couple of precocious kids playing sleepover in a Wes Anderson film, as he explained to me how to use it and we tried not to pass out from heatstroke. We recorded a few small fish, a couple submerged logs, and what may have been a croc – nothing groundbreaking, or even worth including in the episode. Barny watched the budget dedicated to the sonar – renting it, getting trained on using it, shipping it, carrying it with us – slip through his fingers, all for naught. He asked if James could recalibrate it for a larger depth of field, thinking maybe we could get *some* large animal in the distance. We pulled over to the nearest bank under a tall tree so James could work in the shade.

The rest of us got out of the boat and started walking around.

"How do you like the Congo?" asked Ronald.

"Congo? We're in Cameroon, aren't we?" I replied, excited that I could potentially buy a new fridge magnet representing this unexpected foray into a new country.

"We were, but now we are in the Congo."

Laura came over, looking concerned. "Excuse me, did you say the Congo? As in Zaire?"

"Oh, don't say that, it's the Congo now."

"But we can't be in the Congo, we don't have permits or VISAs." Laura was clearly less excited about the promise of a magnet.

"We've been in the Congo all day. This river is the border, we go between the two. Don't worry, no one around here cares. You go from one to the other, it doesn't matter."

"Oh, it does matter, it matters very much! We cannot be in the Congo. If we are in the Congo without a VISA, we can be arrested, or much worse!" The prospect of a Congolese prison was now starting to outweigh the purchase of a magnet.

"No, don't worry. We have money, we cannot be arrested."

"We need to leave immediately. The Congo. We're in the fucking Congo. Barny, did you know we were in the Congo?"

"What? We don't have permits or VISAs! Why are we in the Congo?"

"Oh, the Congo!" said an excited James. "There's some lovely food in the Congo! I didn't know that was on our agenda! I was accused of being a witch the last time I was here."

"Pack it up! We are leaving the Congo!" said Laura. "None of the footage from today can be used! Let's call it a day. The fucking Congo! Really? The Congo isn't exactly a place you want to be in illegally. Jesus, the Congo." (We later found out we'd made numerous forays into the Congo over the past week, which required looking through the footage and determining which shots we were legally able to use.)

We left, jumped back in the boat, grateful to be heading back to our tents and not some terrifying prison, and went back downstream to negotiate our next move. We focused on the area of the river closest to our camp, received assurance that it was all Cameroon, and spent the next five days hanging out with the tribe, hiking into the forest and learning about their legends while they sat around the fire at night, smoked weed, and told stories about the dangers of the forest. Sometimes, these tales came from an elder woman, who started each one with, "Before I had breasts..."

I did feel like I was in the danger zone at times – not in the actual "Danger Zone", which felt remarkably safe, but at different points with the tribe, I felt I was in danger. These tribes lived in rough conditions. They were remarkably happy and incredibly kind, but there was a daily struggle that few Westerners can understand. After leaving one of the villages where we had brought some school supplies and toys, Laura turned to me and said, "I feel like such an ass for worrying about whether to install heated floors in the kitchen of my new flat. I was stressing about it, getting phone calls from the contractor, working it into a budget, right up until the plane took off. It sort of seems as unimportant now as it really is." And that was absolutely the truth. This trip had a way of changing your perception of everything in your life. When you saw people with no worldly possessions and witnessed firsthand the absolute joy they experienced from a life we couldn't imagine, it made you question what we're all doing worrying about getting in line to get the new iPhone. It seems trite or cliched – but it is honestly true. Travel does change you. My internal conflict is far from resolved, but Africa really brought it to the surface. Part of daily life was also dealing with zoological terrors on the scale of... well, Africa. I saw children who couldn't even be two years old receiving instructions on how to kill venomous centipedes that could put a man in hospital from one bite. These would be crawling on the ground, and a man or woman would spot it, pick their baby up and put them in the path of the marauding six-inch bright-red insect. They'd put a stick or knife in the child's hand and direct them how to chop the insect, hitting the head. The child would miss a few times and the pissed-off bug would inch closer. My instinct would be to jump in and help, but I'd hold myself back. Eventually the child would kill it and receive a kiss. I saw one get within about two inches of a kid, to the point where I was convinced the bug was either going to bite her or the kid was going to cut off a toe trying to hit it. This was a life I couldn't imagine.

My nephew and niece, the amazing duo of Nick and Lila, named me Uncle Bug (which was shortened to Bug or Buggy over the years) due to my propensity for taking them outside every time I see them to catch bugs, toads, frogs, snakes, and other creepy crawlers. Upon finding out Anna and I were having a daughter, they immediately christened her "Ladybug". Her real name, Luna, is a type of moth that has always fascinated Anna and me. What I mean by sharing this is that I am no stranger to bugs and no proponent of coddling or shielding kids. I think kids need to get bitten by bugs, scrape their knees, and get dirty. But holy hell, handing a child a machete and putting them in the path of an angry, dangerous arthropod is a different level of experiential teaching and I tried my best not to judge.

Besides the centipedes there were all varieties of snakes, which were killed on sight by the villagers just in case they were venomous – a strategy I would abhor in my native Massachusetts, but one I could see the intrinsic value to here. There were primates, which would alternately steal your food and goods, defecate on you, attack you, or any combination of the three at any given time. While working with gorillas in the Central African Republic, I was charged by a silverback.

Silverback gorillas are one of the most physically intimidating animals on Earth. They are just under six feet tall, around 500 pounds, and have a near nine-foot arm span. They do absolutely whatever they want, at all times, being the definition of "large and in charge". Humans tend to have a visceral reaction to silverbacks – they appear so human but so distinct and intense that an instinct seems to tell us "don't mess with that guy, he'll rip your arms off". No one needs to be told to not poke a silverback. But, like our ancient ancestors, when *Homo sapiens* were the Lewis Skolnick to the other hominins' Ogre, we can't help but think how dimwitted they can appear compared to us nerds. They really can look super dopey, like a very confused cliché of a former HS football player who's gone to seed since his glory days. They even have a beer belly, only theirs isn't filled with natty-ice (bro), but gas from the vegetation they eat all day. This gas also makes them fart, all the time.

They are in some ways like a child who has the physical ability to rip your leg off and beat you to death with it. They wouldn't see why it was wrong to do this because, like a child or a stereotypical jock, if it amuses them or feels good, silverbacks do it. Their forehead ridge, the perpetually furrowed brow and facial expression which reads, "I don't understand and THAT MAKES ME ANGRY!", the belly, the short legs, long arms, and massive chest, the living farting, their sense of entitlement, and the misogyny all scream Hollywood cliche' of a high-school football player. I know, I know – not all football players, but definitely the ones I remember from high school, which taught me that the best way to deal with them was to allow them to think they are the toughest thing around, and show them I know how tough they are, and that I'm not worth paying attention to. Same goes for silverbacks.

The Bayaka pygmy tribe we stayed with located a group of forest gorillas and we were prepped by a research team for an expedition into the forest to observe them. We spent a fair amount of the day before going over safety rules and practices when in the presence of gorillas – safety for the gorillas, that is. Next to nothing was mentioned about how *we* stay safe if a group of animals with near human intelligence, superstrength, and impulse-control issues decided to turn on us. We learned that we should not spit on the gorillas. This would seem to go without saying as all of us were over six years old, but we assumed that it must have been enough of a problem to necessitate a rule about it. In actuality, this was a slight translation error; the rule was not that we couldn't spit *on* the apes, but that we couldn't spit *near* them, or in the forest at all past a certain point. This restored my faith in the researchers who had been there before us.

The viruses in human saliva have decimated some populations of gorilla. Hepatitis in particular has done some really nasty business to their already struggling numbers. We also couldn't bring any food with us for fear we might accidently introduce it into the gorilla's habitat, and to prevent giving the gorillas another reason to attack us. I say "another", because there were already plenty. Gorillas, as a general rule, don't like being observed. They also get jealous easily, are fiercely territorial, and are very protective of their young. We were told not to approach the baby gorillas for any reason. The extent of our "how to not get mauled by a gorilla" talk was, "Don't come between a baby and any adult. And if the silverback charges, don't turn away and don't run, or he will definitely tear you up. Try to lean away from the attack while keeping your feet planted." Basically, pretend you're in *The Matrix*, dodging bullets, only in real life, where instead of bullets it's the claws and two-inch canines of an irrational, jealous, 500 lb. ape who's either showing off and trying to intimidate you, or really wants you gone or dead – either are fine with him.

I had casually studied gorillas before this, as much as any biologist with an interest in primates, and had enough knowledge to be dangerously overconfident. I had worked with young representatives of all great apes, but this was going to be my first time interacting with adult gorillas – and with wild apes at all, in fact. All of my previous experience had been in very controlled settings with captive-raised young apes. Now, we were hiking through the Central African Republic's vast forest with Bayaka pygmies who had a *rough* idea of where the group would be, but where we could encounter a different group of gorillas at any point – who were potentially not as used to human observation as those we were tracking, and more aggressive and defensive.

Any group of gorillas are at first stressed out by the presence of a human – in the words of the researchers, they either "shit themselves and run away or charge at you" as soon as they notice you. This lasts for dozens of encounters, and is actually great for the parasitologists and other researchers who gather gorilla poo and analyze it. There is even research looking into the hormone levels in their poop showing the "fear" hormone decreasing gradually with multiple encounters of the same troop. Some troops never acclimate to human presence while others do, and the shitting and running away or attacking you eventually stops.

The Bayaka have an ancient and ingenious method of tracking the gorillas where one member of their tribe stays with the apes at all times, just out of sight, with a troop who can tolerate their presence reasonably well. The person with the gorillas periodically makes a call which seems to blend with the sounds of the jungle – it alternates between a bird sound, a pig, and a distinct clicking. The rest of the tribe wander in the general direction, listening for the call of their friend, making almost constant click-clack noises with their tongues. The researchers told us this was a sound the gorillas had come to associate with researchers, communicating to them: "We are not a threat."

The tongue clicking announced our presence, as it was nearly impossible to sneak up on them, in the most polite way possible. If they wanted to run, they'd have ample opportunity. The group we were tracking that day was used to being tracked – although this is not to say they were used to or interacted with people, simply that they tolerated people being within sight of them. Even this took years of at least one Bayaka man getting close, then having the gorillas run off, then finding them again the next day, having them run off again, repeated for weeks, then having them spend up to five minutes before they scattered for months, then up to 30 minutes, etc., until eventually they tolerate you being there most of the time. Not large groups, no cameras and equipment, no humans approaching them – just if they caught a whiff of you, or a brief glance, or heard an unfamiliar sound, they wouldn't bolt. We stayed out of sight and downwind as much as possible to be safe and courteous. There was no guarantee they wouldn't take off or the large male silverback wouldn't attack. He had attacked the researchers a few times in the past. That was his job, his purpose – keeping his troop safe.

The silverback (a male who has undergone physiological changes – growing taller and stronger, changing fur color, and sporting an enlarged sagittal crest – in rising to the position of silverback) is the lone sexually active male in a troop. He has a harem of females he mates with and a bunch of young he protects. His only fears in life are losing the reverence, respect, and confidence of his harem, being attacked by humans or leopards, and being killed or beaten by a rival male seeking to become the new silverback. Otherwise, it's a pretty sweet life for the silverback. The one we were tracking was named Makumba, which is both the name of a Central African deity and a phrase meaning "to turn color".

Makumba tolerated people fairly well. He would sometimes "show off" and put on terrifying and threatening displays, but rarely attacked. He could also emit a powerful smell when he felt upset or threatened, or wanted to be particularly intimidating. I'd describe it as a mix of dirty high-school locker-room stink, feces, and something distinctly hormonal – a smell I instinctively knew meant something bad. It was a smell where you got the impression your conscious mind really only took in the surface of it, but you knew there were deeper smells that some recess of your brain was processing. It was more intimidating than his physical appearance, actually, and we are talking about a *massive* animal with huge canines who could outrun and out climb us effortlessly. He had attacked a couple researchers, not causing too much damage. Gorillas rarely killed or maimed researchers – that was a chimp's MO – but they did bite or scratch somewhat frequently, and those bites or scratches would be loaded with all kinds of nasty bacteria and viruses.

Makumba was getting older and had been a silverback for quite a few years. There was a growing fear amongst the researchers that he would be replaced soon, and they'd have to start the painstaking process of gaining the new silverback's trust. This meant there were a few potential rival males in the area, scoping out Makumba's harem. The researchers even thought that one of his females had defected to a different troop a few days before we arrived as she hadn't been seen and there was no sign that she had died. This would be a huge blow to Makumba's ego and might make others in his troop lose faith in him. We were warned he might be more likely to be aggressive or reclusive in light of recent events.

Based on where the gorillas had camped the night before (gorillas are highly nomadic, setting up temporary "nests" of leaves each night and moving on each day), they were somewhere between two and five hours away. The walk was excruciatingly hot and very humid. After about three hours of profuse sweating, battling lots of bees, mosquitoes, biting flies, and massive nests of social spiders – each containing thousands of the arachnids and encasing good portions of trees – and the constant fear of running into an unknown group of gorillas or, worse, a lone male, our clicking guides heard the call of the Bayaka who was with the troop. We waited while a researcher went ahead. She came back about 20 minutes later with mixed news. Makumba was in a bad mood. Not bad enough to attack us, but not good enough to allow us all there, she thought. We'd have to go in groups of two. Despite not showering for days, not wearing any sunscreen, bug repellent, deodorant, or any chemical scent, she was worried too many of us would smell too foreign to the troop and "something bad will happen". Since we didn't want something bad to happen, we agreed. We also agreed that when she said to leave, we would leave – no arguments, no "one more shot". Leave. She had clearly worked with film crews before and knew our ways.

I was in the first group – it was going to be just Duncan and me with the researcher and Bayaka guides. We were instructed how to click as we walked. It felt like we had barely left the others when suddenly there were about five adult female gorillas and double that number of babies and juveniles all around us. I looked up, we *had* barely left them – I could still see James and a very concerned-looking Barny through the trees. Makumba was nowhere in sight, but he had to be close by. I realized quickly that we were *way* too close to the females, and because of their movements I was directly between some of them and the juveniles. I don't want to say I panicked, but I was literally doing one of the few things we had been instructed not to do. All I had to do now was stare down Makumba and spit on one of the others to complete my transgressions. As a female walked towards me with conviction, a researcher hissed, "Don't move and don't make eye contact! Look away."

"But she's looking right at me."

"She can look at you, you can't look at her. God, she shouldn't be looking at you either. Where is Makumba? This is bad."

I quickly feigned absolute fascination in a leaf on the tree near me and could only see the female in my peripheral vision. She walked within inches of me, stopped for a minute, reached up like she might touch me, decided better of it, and moved on. The researcher quickly got the message to Barny and the others. "Move back, now. Move far back." I saw James' blonde hair and ever-present Tilley hat disappearing behind the trees and realized the crisis had been averted.

And then Makumba ambled into view. He was massive. All of the gorillas were, actually. At first I thought it was the fear of not having any glass between me and them which made them seem larger than gorillas in the zoo, but was later told that wild gorillas are in fact larger due to their diets. Makumba moved with such grace and confidence that you couldn't help but respect him immediately. He didn't have the dopey look of a gorilla that we might think of when looking at a photo. He looked like an apex predator and a thinking, well-composed soldier. When he flopped on the ground to sit, it seemed to shake with his weight. I was shocked to see him climb trees effortlessly. In one fluid movement, apparently expending no energy, Makumba would be 30 feet up a tree dropping branches for his troop to pick through and eat the leaves, stems, fruits, and seeds, and he climbed down just as easily and quickly. It's hard to express how disconcerting it was to see him move so fast, and to see an animal that top heavy climb a tree like that. He noticed us watching him and I averted my eyes, to which he grunted a "humpf" and went back to eating. He appeared totally calm, laying on his back and playing with an infant. The baby was climbing onto his belly then jumping off. If the baby stumbled Makumba would pick it up and place it back on his stomach, then the game would continue. He seemed like a contented dad. As trite and cliche as it is to say, I've played the same game with my kids dozens of times and recognized the behavior immediately. It was completely surreal.

The young gorillas were so much like small children that it was easy to forget that they weren't, in fact, humans. They played, ran around, seemed to dare each other to get closer to us, and were just having a great time being kids, all under the watchful eyes of a little over a dozen females. Our researcher chaperone seemed to relax as we were a good distance away and Makumba hadn't done anything rash, so the coast was clear for us to film. We shot a little with the juveniles playing behind me – they would climb up to the broken point of a fallen tree (about 10 feet up), then bellyflop into a pile of leaves and branches. They waited in line to do this, one after the other. It was hysterical. They would also wait until one of us was watching before jumping. You could almost hear them saying, "Hey, Mister! Mister! Look at me! Watch what I can do!" I could have watched them all day, but we had a few other shots to get. Almost as soon as we turned our attention to Makumba he became agitated, made a few gut-wrenching-scary grunts, threw some leaves, and bolted. The females and juveniles followed. Maybe it was my imagination, but they seemed reluctant, like they wanted to stay and show off for us. We looked at the researcher who seemed a bit conflicted, but after biting her lip for a few seconds said, "Okay, let's follow, but stay behind me." We did. We followed for about a mile, through dense forest, crossing shallow streams, and going up and down hills. We got glimpses of the troop ahead of us, but not much more.

Then, when we were crossing a wide and shallow stream, we heard a scream, a growl, and saw Makumba charging towards us, mouth open, teeth barred, and splashing the water violently with his huge arms. He was about 200 feet away and closing in fast. Every instinct I had was to turn and run, but a very small part of my brain reminded me what a terrible idea that would be. I saw Makumba's obviously angry face and remembered how fast and effortlessly he moved when he wanted to. This charge was not meant to harm us, but intimidate us. He was splashing too much, making too much of a display. If he'd wanted to attack he'd have done so before my brain had had the time to process it. This was a threat, nothing more. I looked down and fumbled with the strap on my bag, pretending to play with it, eat it, stare at it, like you would a super-interesting blade of grass. I was trying, with all of my body language, to say, "Nothing to see here, just interested in this strap. You are the biggest and toughest thing around and I know it. I am humbled before your power." It was the equivalent to pretending to read a book when a bully walked by in grade school, and it worked just as well. Makumba stopped, grunted, splashed one more time, and walked away.

"What the fuck happened?" was all Duncan could say to the researcher.

"I have no idea, that was *really* interesting, though. And intense. We'll have to talk to the guys and figure it out later." It turned out that one of the potential rival males was nearby (none of us saw him, but the guides did), and one of Makumba's harem checked him out, glancing over at him and apparently sizing him up. This enraged Makumba – he looked at it as losing face in front of us. He threw her into a tree (the scream we heard), then charged at us to let us know he was still in control. We got the message, agreed with it, and all was right with the world again.

As mentioned before, Duncan had seen some things on his travels, and was fairly unflappable. He showed me his hand after Makumba's charge and it was shaking like a leaf. Duncan is a ruggedly handsome, tall, older British man who somehow looks exactly like you imagine a British cameraman for wildlife documentaries should look. He doesn't smoke regularly, but looks like a hand-rolled cigarette should be hanging out of his mouth all the time, or at least in a black-and-white photo where he's wearing army fatigues, a bandana, and an unbuttoned shirt with epaulettes. He is effortlessly cool and still dad-like. He's very kind, but tough as nails and taught me a lot about hosting, which would be interesting to exactly 0.1% of the folks reading this, but it was invaluable. He also scared me a few times, which I learned I really like in a cameraman.

The troop stopped shortly after and resumed their normal activities – grooming each other, eating, playing, etc. We felt guilty spending as much time with them as we were, so after we got all of the B-roll we could justify we went back to tag in the rest of the crew, who were able to spend another hour or so observing before the researchers said it was best to call it a day. The faces of the young gorillas waiting in line to show off will stay with me for the rest of my life, as will the image of Makumba's bared teeth as he charged at me. It was possibly the only time in my life I've been in danger and actually responded in the correct way.

There were other less dramatic animal encounters in the villages – there was a goat who screamed like a person. If I had thought to record it, it would have been a YouTube sensation. There was also a rooster that we hated so much that James and I began offering a reward to anyone willing to kill it. I had a pug and, due to his snores and snuffles, slept with earplugs in for all of his 16 years, but these earplugs in for the past 14 years, but these earplugs did nothing to muffle the noise of this disgusting bird that would start its call at about 4:30am – over an hour before any other rooster. It was the loudest, most annoying sound I've ever heard an animal make. It sounded diseased – I think his throat was raw and infected from calling so loudly, and the rooster himself was *enormous*. He was a white-and-black beast that was missing most of his feathers, often seen picking a fight with any other animal near him and forcing himself on the terrified hens at every opportunity. I hated that rooster, and we would talk about cooking it. James made the unfortunate mistake of commenting on how "delicious that cock would be" – a comment he will never be able to live down, despite its accuracy and literal correctness.

There were also less obvious dangers in West Africa. There are things I'm not great at, even at home – social expectations and societal norms. Most cultures are very forgiving of the accidental foibles of stupid Westerners. Cross a hearth of a nomad's ger (Yurt to Westerners – another faux pas) and you are stating that you would like to come between him and his wife. Point your shoe at someone in the Middle East – well, we've all seen the "shoe thrown at President Bush" video by now. Most of these were laughed off after a quick explanation from the fixers to the offended parties, then the perplexed Westerner, generally accompanied by many apologies, and sometimes with a token gift.

One night, the Baka village threw a party for us. There was LOTS of palm wine and weed (we did not partake in either), dancing, music played on traditional instruments, and singing. It was a fun time for all. We basically stayed on the fringes and watched, smiling, laughing, and enjoying the entire scene. A person covered entirely in flowing palm leaves with no part of their body visible suddenly appeared in the dance circle. The costume made them look like Cousin It, but we were told by the guides that it was a mischievous forest spirit. The "spirit" seemed to be enjoying itself and was gyrating and grabbing women, only to be pushed away by the laughing men of the village. The women would turn away from "his" advances as well, laughing and dancing. I was dragged from the sidelines and invited to join in and help "banish" the spirit back to the forest. I tried mimicking the movements of the other men as much as possible, but I'm a terrible dancer and pretty uncoordinated. The entire village seemed to be laughing at my attempts and I was laughing with them. I made a few missteps and had my hands slapped when I tried mimicking the guy next to me in touching the palm fronds, but apparently when I did this it was taboo. Partially because I wasn't a member of the tribe, and partially the way I did it was evidently inviting the spirit into the village.

James reminded me that this may look like fun, and the villagers were in good spirits with all the drinks and weed, but I really shouldn't mess with any of the "spirits" – "If anyone gets hurt tonight or wakes up sick, we don't want this to come back to you inviting a spirit in, mate. Best to just sit back, I reckon." In a village where malaria was common and often struck without warning, I heeded his advice and went back to the sidelines, content to just clap along to the beat. A few minutes later, a very drunk woman grabbed my hands and pulled me to the circle again. She wanted to dance and wouldn't take no for an answer.

She was probably in her forties, almost five feet tall, and was lean and muscular. She was missing quite a few teeth and the ones she had were filed to points. She had elaborate facial and hand tattoos, and was wearing a white calf-length summer dress. She held my hands and tried to lead me in a traditional dance, then, when she saw I was hopeless, grabbed my butt and forced me to sway. Everyone around us was howling with laughter. She would mimic my terrible "white-man dance", then laugh and grab my butt or hips again. I tried "skanking" – just about the only dance move I'm even remotely comfortable with from my ska days. This produced significantly more laughter and mimicking. Even the kids were getting into it now. A few women dragged my dance partner away, motioning that they were sorry and she was drunk. I laughed and made a "no worries!" gesture. I danced with a few little kids next, as long as I was up and already embarrassing myself. We were laughing and dancing and having fun when my drunk partner came back. Like a lot of drunk women I have come across, "She just wanted to dance. Why won't you let her dance, guys? She's honestly totally fine and really, really, *really* just wants to dance." And dance with me she did. There was gyrating, and hip shaking, and laughing, and hoots and hollers. It went on for about 10 more minutes before the same friends showed up, apologized again, and dragged her away. She hugged me quick, slapped my stomach, and blew me kisses as they dragged her off. I took a bow, everyone cheered and clapped, and the party kept going.

When I left the dance floor, Ronald walked up to me. "That was very funny, I think they enjoyed that very much."

"I'm glad! I had fun too. I'm not much of a dancer but that was really a good time."

"You did a good job, you should be proud. You know you're married now, right? In this culture, when you dance like that, it's a marriage ritual."

"What? What do you mean?" I was pretty sure he was kidding, but he wasn't smiling, and Ronald wasn't a big joker.

"Yes, you didn't know? I thought we went over this before the party." Okay, this was sounding terrifyingly plausible. Ronald had gone over a bunch of do's and don'ts, but we were all so tired. I remembered the ones that seemed important, I thought.

"No, no what do you mean? How do I fix this?"

"Fix this? Why, she is very nice. She is very drunk, though. I wonder if that will matter?"

Just as the horrifying reality of this was starting to sink in, Ronald broke into a huge smile and started laughing: "You should have seen your face! Hahahahah!"

He then told the story to the other guides who found it equally hysterical. Once I started breathing again, I did too. It was a damn good prank, and the dangers of accidently marrying a woman were certainly more real and terrifying than the Danger Zone.

The day we were to get back out on the water of the forbidden-danger-zone arrived too quickly. It was another scorcher and we all knew that we needed some sonar footage to justify the expense. We spent another full day in the Danger Zone that went much like the first and yielded no footage at all. Finally, around dusk, after the tenth power outage due to hitting the bottom, Barny called it. "Screw it. Let's just collect the camera traps and hope we've got something worth seeing on them." The sonar wouldn't be spoken of again, except in hushed tones proceeded by various obscenities, and never in Barny's presence.

The first five traps were a bust – nothing but insects, leaves, and a couple small birds. The next ones were in the Congo and couldn't have been used even if we had caught anything good, but we didn't. The final two were on the island we had explored, the one that seemed to be in the most isolated part of the river. I started going through the pictures, but we were all exhausted. We were dripping sweat, sunburned, hadn't eaten in hours, and were getting slap-happy. I was stumbling over my words and we kept having to reshoot because of flubbed lines or one of us laughing.

"C'mon, guys, just a bit more and we're done for the day. Please just say the stupid words." "Butt-hole," said James, which was our current favorite "stupid word" and prompted another fit of laughter and more wasted time. Children – we all turn into children on these shoots.

"Okay, sorry, Barny. For real, I've got it, I'm ready." I turned to the camera, still rolling. "We're on this island in the middle of the Danger Zone, about to check a camera trap we left here about a week ago. It's in a perfect area to catch a large animal who may be using this island as a basking spot or a refuge from the deeper and faster waters around here. Let's see what we've got. (Picture 1) Nothing. (Pictures 2-27) Bird, leaf, fly, nothing, bird, etc. (Picture 28) Wow. Um…" I started giggling, then laughing harder, progressing into shaking fits of uncontrolled laughter. I tried to stifle it and pull myself together. "Phew. Well… it's a… There's just a guy in a bikini." James starts to break while even Duncan cracks a smirk, and I see the camera shake imperceptibly as he stifles his laughter.

The image on the 2.5-inch screen was that of a young, strong, African man in teeny-tiny, forest green, bikini-briefs. He's confidently striding, Sasquatch like, with his arms swinging, across the frame, barefoot. The impending heat exhaustion, combined with the surrealism of this image, hit my humor nail right on the head. This was *Aqua Teen Hunger Force* bizarre and I loved it. I showed the image to the camera and Duncan broke: "There's a man in his pants!" Then everyone lost it. James and Laura started concocting stories about how this man ended up in the Danger Zone in just his pants. The group favorite involved multiple lovers, human and mythical, seducing him on the island after luring him to it, siren-style.

After that, Barny agreed to call it a day. "We're done. Let's leave this place. We'll figure out what to do with the footage. Arnold, what the Hell man? Danger Zone? Danger for whom? From What? There's a guy walking confidently in his pants, for God's sake. We're supposed to be in the middle of nowhere, a no-man's land, THE DANGER ZONE."

Arnold looked crushed. "Ah yes, there are more people here than usual, I guess. They must know Mokele M'bembe is hibernating."

We all started laughing then, even Barny. Arnold was *still* selling it. Fixers – you have to love them, even when you passionately hate them. We had found absolutely no evidence of any unknown animal, no evidence that a dinosaur had ever lived in this region, no signs of danger in the danger zone, but Arnold was sticking by it. I learned a few things in those days on the river. I learned how much sweat my body could produce. I learned that fixers make a living from people wanting to visit their location, so they sometimes exaggerate the features of the places they serve as guides for. And I learned that the only danger in the Danger Zone is being in the Congo illegally with men wearing bikini briefs.

Chapter 5

Mokele M'bembe — Not Cool, Science, Not Cool

Hello there and thank you for making it this far with me. We've come to the "cryptid", or mysterious animals that may or may not exist, chapter of the book. This is either a very weird turn in the funny travel book you've been enjoying, or you were *very* confused by the first few chapters of the cryptozoology book you purchased. I will not be citing my sources here (most of them are my own notes and memories anyway). Feel free to Google anything I mention and write angry e-mails and nasty tweets about how I got the tributaries of the Congo River mixed up with each other. This is not a paper in a scientific journal, it's a collection of true stories from my personal experiences and some of my opinions. When making *Beast Hunter* we needed to cite at least two credited (peer-reviewed or expert-opinion) sources for every fact I stated on camera. There was a fact checker at Nat Geo whose job was to pick apart every line said. Most networks do not require this, but it's one of the reasons I love Nat Geo so much, and why Nat Geo is among the most respected brands in the world. This did make our job of making films about animals that may or may not exist very difficult. There were so many retakes in order to throw in a "perhaps" or a "some experts say" that we ended up doing a five-minute reel of me just repeating phrases that imply ambiguity in different intonations which we could cut in during editing. Realistically, we loved the scrutiny and I feel it made the series much better than your run-of-the-mill crypto show filled with statements like "that's definitely a werewolf" when someone hears a barred owl; or an episode with more night-vision footage than a wannabe actor's "break-out" video (regardless of whether the proposed animal is nocturnal or not) and lots of loud noises and Blair Witch-style nausea-inducing camera movements followed by, "What's *THAT?!?*", or – in my opinion, the biggest crime in this field – faked news stories or actors playing scientists.

There were a few things in *Beast Hunter* that were cut by our fact checker which I would still argue were true. We lost a whole segment when I caught a hagfish because I said, "They aren't closely related to anything else, and they really aren't even a fish by strict definition." I *may* have slightly overstated how different they are evolutionarily, but I maintain that what I said was true. My friend Zeb, a marine biologist, is probably cringing reading this. But it's that kind of scrutiny and adherence to the truth that I think set our show apart. Anyway, there is no fact checker on this book, other than you, dear reader. So check away, but, as I said, these are mostly my own thoughts, opinions, and experiences.

In case you haven't figured it out yet, I am a nerd. Not like a "I have a *Star Wars* shot glass" nerd – like a real nerd. Specifically, a science nerd. This differs from the so-hot-right-now comic book/sci-fi nerd. Sure, I liked *Fringe* as much as the next guy, I've read all of the *Song of Ice and Fire* books to date, and my high-school friends and I stayed in on Friday nights to watch *The X-Files*, but my true nerd status really becomes apparent whenever a conversation strays into any topic in biology.

I advocated for the name "Darwin" if our first child was a boy, and when we found out we were having a daughter I tried to convince Anna it would still make a great middle name. We ended up naming her Luna after the amazingly beautiful and mysterious *Actias luna*, the luna moth. Yes, I'm aware that Luna Lovegood is a character in one of my favorite book series – she's one of Anna's and my favorite characters, in fact, but that's an added bonus for the name rather than a driving force. Our son is named Wallace Charles after Alfred Russel Wallace, Charles Darwin, and Charles Fort.

I was a teaching assistant for multiple chemistry and biology labs and audited extra biology and philosophy classes – for fun. I traveled to Maryland to observe horseshoe crabs mating – again, for fun. One of the only real fights I can remember getting into with my best friend since birth was when we were eight and he insisted that crabs were amphibians. The only TV shows I watched in the eighties and nineties were nature programs. Whenever I was sick and off school I was allowed to rent anything I wanted from the video store. My pick was always a volume of *Life on Earth*. David Attenborough, Alfred Russel Wallace, and Charles Darwin were my childhood heroes, and remain my adult heroes – in addition to Harry Marshall, the founder and head of Icon Films and the man responsible for sending me on all of these adventures and forever changing the course of my life. He also makes damn fine TV.

When I left home at 16 and lived on my own for the first time it was for a marine biology internship in Maine. A friend asked what the nightlife was like in southern Maine. I replied, with no hesitation or sense of irony, "Great! It's really awesome! There are foxes, raccoons, lightning bugs, polyphemus moths, and so far I've spotted two species of owls!" I also read the *Fortean Times* and *CryptoZooNews*, and most of the people I follow on social media are naturalists. Don't worry, though – I won't get *too* scientific in this chapter (and there will be poop jokes).

I say all of this because, in recent years, there has been a move towards hijacking nerd culture by moderately cool people. An actor who can't quite cut it turns to fantasy shows and suddenly he's a heartthrob. A few years back, even Charlie Sheen "led a search for the Loch Ness Monster". I happened to be in Scotland, investigating the same monster at the same time he was, and heard some horror stories from the locals about his behavior in their beautiful country. I am not a person who does this stuff for the attention – I do it because I love it and am fascinated by it, and because I think it doesn't do science any favors to simply write off the things that sound bizarre.

Too many scientists forget that the general public does not consist primarily of other scientists, and most people would rather hear about the *possibility* of a bipedal intelligent ape walking around the Great North Woods than the reality of the new barnacle you discovered. Run with that – talk about the *possibility*. It will get people listening. Then you can throw in some stuff about wolverines, the reintroduction of wolves, and pine martens. Make it something that people, real people, will find interesting. Throw in some jokes, give some sexy facts – more people will be interested in your lame barnacle if you lead with the fact that it has the largest penis-to-body ratio of any animal in the world. It's over six times the total length of its body! That's CRAZY! And fascinating! And memorable. Where do they keep it? How do ... I'm getting sidetracked, the point is — don't refuse to talk about something because you think it sounds silly. Getting people outside for a homemade Bigfoot expedition still gets them outside, and they *will* see other amazing and exciting things, even if they don't see a sasquatch. A generation of Bigfoot hunters might turn into conservationists, or field biologists, or maybe lawyers who want to protect the land they loved exploring as a kid. Another interesting side effect of not immediately writing these things off, all of you closed-minded scientists out there, is that sometimes, *sometimes*, you might find that there is actually *something* to these stories. If you go out there, use your scientific training, open your mind, dispel disbelief and really look at the facts and evidence. You might surprise yourself, like I did with Orang Pendek and others.

I'm an open-minded skeptic at heart, and I approached everything around *Beast Hunter* as such. There's a famous quote regarding Occam's razor that goes something like: "When you hear hoof beats in the distance, you don't think it's a herd of unicorns. You think of horses, and you're probably correct." I also think of horses, but am willing to be shown the evidence of unicorns. I did have a "mistaken identity" theory for each cryptid in the series; however, I was more interested in the cultural significance of each myth than its veracity.

In the world of cryptozoology, Mokele M'bembe (MM) has some of the most ardent supporters. I suspect that some of this devotion is due to the fact that MM is supposedly a living dinosaur species – and there isn't a kid I know who didn't go through a dinosaur phase. At some point in everyone's life, they desperately want to believe that somewhere, somehow, dinosaurs survived. When Westerners hear, "There's supposedly a species of long-necked dinosaur that survived in the swamps and rivers of Congo, Cameroon, and the Central African Republic," that childhood desire and fascination meld with the very little that you probably know about those countries in "mysterious Africa", and you think, "That just might be possible – that doesn't sound completely insane." But most Westerners are not biologists, and most have not been to West Africa.

Stories of MM reached the West in the early 1900s and caused a media sensation. Some famous explorers came back from the jungles of Africa with tall tales about a menagerie of dinosaur-like creatures. Newspapers took the accounts at face value and published exaggerated tales about these beasts. No proof of their existence was ever produced, but the stories captured people's imaginations and fueled the sense of mystery and wonder that Africa inspired.

I will admit, when I first discussed the MM expedition with Harry Marshall, head of the production company Icon, we were both a little hesitant. We both agreed that it was a really interesting story and worth an investigation, but also that if there *was* anything behind the stories it was almost certainly not a living sauropod-like dinosaur. This encapsulated the real challenge of the series – how to present a very unscientific hypothesis (a living dinosaur going undocumented in equatorial West Africa) in a scientific way. We had decided that this series was not *MythBusters*. We were not looking to disprove the existence of any animal, but at the same time we had to maintain scientific credibility. After a quick discussion, I suggested dropping it and going for a different cryptid. What about another "living relic" – maybe the thylacine or Megalania in Australia? Or a more unique location? What about the Yeti in Bhutan? Harry thought those were already too documented, too recent, and too believable. *Beast Hunter* was to follow in Charles Fort's tradition – we were supposed to thumb our nose at accepted opinions, be provocative, present hypotheses that mainstream science would laugh off, and then make them question whether they pooh-poohed it too quickly. We were supposed to be the finger in the eye of the establishment.

"What do *you* think Mokele M'bembe is?" I remember Harry asking.

"In that part of the world, I guess it could be anything," was my reply.

Harry's eyes lit up. "Exactly, it could be *anything*." We decided this, more than any of the other episodes, would be an exercise in objective evidence gathering. Nearly every MM expedition in the modern era had an agenda to prove that a species of dinosaur is still living, which influenced everything they did. We would go in with no preconceived notions. Nothing to prove, no strong hypothesis, just one fact – people have reported seeing a large animal in the lakes, streams, and swamps of this region for centuries, and they call this animal Mokele M'bembe, the one who stops the flow of rivers.

I'm going to do the same here – present the evidence, the facts, the results, and give my thoughts on them. If this chapter hasn't already pissed off a lot of people, it certainly will as you read on. Sorry for that – the episode of *Beast Hunter* pissed a lot of people off too. Harry, Nat Geo, and I agreed that we would make this as real as we could and present what we found. I also wanted to write this book as honestly as I could, and that includes facts I wish were not true. I want there to be a living dinosaur in the world, of course, but all the evidence pointed in a different direction. Also, when I say "dinosaur" I mean it in the same way an eight-year-old does – a badass ancient animal. I know that some of the animals I mention (like plesiosaurs) are not dinosaurs – in that case they are Mesozoic marine reptiles – don't @ me bro.

If you search for Mokele M'bembe on the interwebs, you will find a very interesting thing about many of its most ardent supporters. A lot of folks promoting its existence are from a particular branch of evangelical Christians who seem to believe that finding a living dinosaur would both disprove evolution and prove a perplexing bit of faith-based "science" called "Young Earth Creationism" (YEC), the belief that the Earth is less than 10,000 years old. Depending on the survey, between 10 and 40 percent of American's believe this.

When asked for evidence for their belief in a young Earth, these folks point to the Bible, which does not come out and say how old the Earth is. By calculating the genealogies of the main characters in the Torah, however, they've come up with creation occurring between six and ten thousand years ago. The Bible has, to be generous, a few scientific inaccuracies, so I'd like to think that most people agree it's best to be read more as a spiritual guide and less as a science textbook if they believe it should be read at all.

I will not present the evidence to contradict the claims of YECs. If you are considering the merits of YEC's beliefs but do not have access to a reputable peer-reviewed journal, textbook, or a college-level class on the subject of geology, physical geography, carbon dating or the like, please pick up Richard Dawkins' amazing work *The Greatest Show on Earth*, wherein he succinctly presents "old Earth" evidence that is easily digestible for non-scientists, and does so in one chapter.

What I really struggle with in regard to YEC and MM, though, is the fact that a living dinosaur would neither disprove evolution nor prove a young Earth. There are numerous species of plants and animals alive today which are virtually indistinct from their prehistoric ancestors – coelacanths, dawn redwoods, velvet worms, and horseshoe crabs have been around for tens or hundreds of millions of years in nearly the same form that we see today. This actually helps prove evolution by natural selection (these animals all do a great job at doing what they do and surviving, they have no pressures to change and are not working towards some "higher design", and so are not changing), and has absolutely no bearing on the age of the Earth. In fact, horseshoe crabs are *older* than any dinosaur – appearing over 400 million years ago to dinosaurs' 200 million. So why the appearance of a living *younger* (compared to horseshoe crabs) animal species would change our scientifically-proven facts I can't wrap my head around. All that aside, I guess the thought of riding a velociraptor is pretty awesome, and I can understand hoping that could have happened at some point.

I say all of this not to mock anyone's beliefs, but to show that *Beast Hunter* is one of the few investigations into MM without an agenda. We weren't looking to prove something larger with its existence, or lack of. We weren't even trying to prove that it existed, or did not. We were looking into the veracity of the claims, objectively observing the evidence, and seeing the cultural significance of the story.

I also want to say again that *Beast Hunter* was as real as a TV show can be. We didn't fake anything, plant any evidence, falsify data, or tell anyone to say anything. Each episode was over 15 days of filming condensed into around 45 minutes of airtime, so there is far more you don't see than you do. When talking to villagers, a lot of the conversations didn't go anywhere, directly contradicted the evidence we presented, led us down a different path, or seemed to fit so well that it was as if we scripted it. We tried to always show this, but for every conversation you saw there were a dozen similar ones. For instance, there is a shot of me walking around the market in Yokadouma, Cameroon asking about MM where a person shakes their head, indicating they have never heard of it. This is about two seconds of footage – in reality, there were probably 20 of those same interactions. Then we find a woman who says, "Go to the Baka, they know about this animal," which was word for word what we had in our script and what we hoped to hear, and it happened, with no prompting, three or four times.

We also had a lot of people tell us things about MM that didn't fit with the narrative of the show, so they weren't included. This is true of every scene where we approach strangers in every episode. It's not that we ever misled the audience, it's just we can't show everything, so we focus on what's important to the story. If we had someone say, "C'mon! That's ridiculous, no one believes that! It's all for show for the tourists!", we would have included it — we genuinely would have. What I mean by "didn't fit with the narrative" is sometimes people would go in a completely different direction that would be too timely to explore – "MM is the ghost of our ancestors," "MM is a demon," etc. These could be fascinating to explore, but we just didn't have the time, so we concentrated on the cases that fit the broad narrative, such as one person who has never heard of MM, and one person who has. In reality, we probably had 20 who had never heard of it, another six who had heard something that didn't help us (like that it has a huge trunk, similar to an elephant), and eight who had heard of a giant dinosaur-like creature.

When I asked about mysterious animals, one woman described an "evil" animal they had dug up, alive, a few weeks ago: "It had no fur, and long slashing claws. Its face was terrifying and it made horrible noises. Its wrinkled skin looked like it was rotting and it had a rat's tail." I realized early on that she was describing an aardvark, but let her go on to solidify the point that people extrapolate, exaggerate, and assume things about a creature they have never seen before. This made it into the first edit of the episode, but was eventually cut as we made this point with another "eyewitness" to MM.

I hope all of this is making sense, and that after reading it you have a better understanding of the editing process for a show like this. There was never an intention to mislead, only a time crunch driving the decisions into what shots to include or cut. I 100% stand by everything in every episode. So, with all of that said, onto the evidence – and an in-depth look at whether it really constitutes "evidence" at all.

"The locals from different regions of central and western equatorial Africa who have no contact with each other always identify a picture of a sauropod as Mokele M'bembe."

One of the legends around MM touted to prove its existence and identity it as a dinosaur goes as follows: "When the local tribes are shown pictures of sauropods, they identify them as Mokele M'bembe." A quick online search will show you that this is not true, but it continues to be used as "proof" of a living dinosaur so I'll tackle it and hopefully put it to bed for good. First off, "local people" are not one group. They are from different tribes with vastly different traditions and customs, speak different languages, and have divergent accounts of MM. Some say there are multiple different dinosaur species: sauropod-like, protoceratops-like, ceratopsian-like, etc., all with different local names; sometimes, in one tribe, the name for the protoceratops-like creature will be the same as the sauropod-like creature in another tribe, and the name of a known animal (like an elephant) in a third tribe. This makes for any attempt at classification very difficult, and interviewing eyewitnesses almost impossible. You could (and we did) experience something like the following:

Tribe member: "I have seen Mokele M'bembe."

MM researcher: "Great! Can you describe it?"

"Like a rhino, but with six horns and a large back-plate behind its head."

"Do you mean Ngoubou?"

"No, Ngoubou is a rhino. This was like a rhino, but with..."

"Yes, six horns and a plate. Do you mean Njago-gunda?"

"No, Njago-gunda is like a hippo, but with a large horn and strong tail."

"That sounds like Chipekwe."

"Chipekwe is smaller than Emela-ntouka, larger than a rhino, and has a longish neck, short legs, and a tail with bony plates that stand two feet tall in rows down its back with spikes on the end of its tail."

"Okay, so what is Emela-ntouka?"

"Emela-ntouka is a huge beast, as big as three elephants, with a long tail and neck and very large spikes like spear-heads running down the length of its long neck, back, and tail."

"Yes, that one! Well, I've never heard the spikes part, but sounds good, close enough. Have you seen Emela-ntouka?"

"No, no one living has, they all died in my grandfather's grandfather's time."

"Okay, well, back to Mokele M'bembe, that still sounds very interesting and dinosaur-like..."

It would seem from looking at all of the eyewitness accounts that Cameroon, the Congo, and the Central African Republic constitute a veritable Jurassic Park, yet no photos – even blurry "blobsquatch" photos – of any of these dinosaurs have surfaced, despite many of our guides carrying smartphones in 2010, and their being even more prevalent now. The names really are tricky to pronounce – not as hard to say as some in Mongolian, but pretty tough, and very hard to keep track of. I had a spreadsheet of each name for a "sauropod-like creature" in every language and every region we went to. I won't list all of them. If you're interested in a fairly exhaustive list, numerous books have been written on the subject. Be forewarned, though

– my experiences are *vastly* different to most researchers who have travelled there. On the topic of MM however, I do highly recommend Coleman's *The Field Guide to Lake Monsters, Sea Serpents, and Other Mystery Denizens of the Deep* – it's a fun read, and definitely informative.

If you get past the names and just go with "locals pick out a photo of a sauropod as *an* animal they have seen", it still seems that each researcher has performed the photo experiment in their own way since it was first reported in the 1920s, and the way an experiment or survey question (as this experiment kind of is) is structured matters. Think about the statement I made about YEC earlier, that between 10 and 40 percent of Americans believe in it. That's a huge variation – a difference of about 100 million people. That huge variation in response comes primarily from how the question is worded. Check out an article in the National Center for Science Education entitled "Just How Many Young-Earth Creationists Are There in the U.S.?" for more info on this specifically, or look into any political poll. Any survey can easily be made to favor one side or the other by the way the questions are asked. Wording and the setup of an experiment matter.

Some researchers have shown tribe members a selection of drawings and asked, "Which one of these is Mokele M'bembe?" to which the majority of interviewees allegedly pick a picture of a dinosaur. This is a flawed experiment for a number of reasons. It presupposes that the animal exists, that the people being polled have heard of it and have seen it, and that they have seen and know all of the other animals which might be confused for MM which they are shown pictures of. Put yourself in the position of an indigenous person – you are shown photos of 15 animals and asked which one is MM. If you've never seen or heard about MM before, you can simply pick the picture of the animal you've never seen. Now, you might say, "But the researchers threw in a mix of images of local animals and ones they knew the tribes wouldn't be familiar with." Okay, let's assume that's true – which is a big assumption without actually seeing the set of drawings – and that these are folks who don't get a lot of visitors. There are all of these crazy Westerners causing a commotion and asking about this animal – if you've never heard of it before, you've probably heard *something* about it by the time you get to the picture round. Again, let's make a huge assumption and say foreigners show up in your remote Cameroonian village, and the first thing they do is show you a series of drawings of known and unknown animals and ask you which one is Mokele M'bembe – two words you've never heard before. You eliminate all of the animals you recognize – well that's an elephant, a rhino, a hippo, a gorilla, a rat, a crocodile, a python, and so on. You're left with a few images of bizarre-looking creatures. You're probably thinking, "These Westerners didn't come here to find that tiny animal that looks like an armored pig, I'm guessing they want me to pick the biggest, most badass-looking animal out there," so you pick one of the dinosaur options. They are excited! They are happy! These crazy people.

Now, let's be realistic – this is not your opening move. You don't meet a tribe in a remote region of the Congo and immediately jump to "pick a card". There are customs to follow, greetings that must occur, niceties to observe. You chat for a while, establish trust, and determine if they even know about this animal. Let's completely forget the above scenario – of course the people you are asking have heard of MM, you wouldn't be there if they hadn't, you would have established that they had never heard of it and moved on down the river to the next village. So they have heard of it, but have they seen it? Have you ever seen a dragon? After hearing one detailed fairy tale about one, would you be able to pick the picture of a dragon out of a series of images of animals? Of course you would. Even so, the stories go that most people picked the picture of the dinosaur – most, not all. This means that even with the cards stacked so far in the favor of picking a dinosaur, some people still picked the warthog.

"This is Mokele M'bembe – look at its wide, fearsome jaws, bulging eyes, and horrific, twisted shape."

"Nope, that's my pug. His name is Sushi. Next villager please."

The above version would be great to do if there was no picture of a dinosaur in the mix, with the researcher asking, "Which of these is MM?", and using a control group, then see if the control group always picks the biggest animal, or the weirdest-looking one. As far as I know, this has never been done. Based on what I saw in West Africa, the kind people in the villages would want to please and pick a picture, telling you it was MM no matter what.

Other researchers have asked the question in a slightly better way. They show the villagers a series of images and for each one ask, "Can you name this animal?" This seems logical, reasonable, and has a built-in control to see if they are lying or guessing. I used this technique. This produces far worse results than the first method, as you may have guessed. When a picture of an American bison popped up, for instance, the locals looked intrigued.

"I don't know what that is."

Excellent, I thought. They're not lying. This is great.

"Elephant."

Yup, got it.

"Python."

Anaconda, but close enough, got it.

"Mokele M'bembe."

Great, they picked the sauropod.

"Hippo."

Yup, got it.

The next image draws hesitation from the crowd. "I don't know what that is."

Odd, it's a rhino. They must not have ever seen one. Okay, moving on.

"Gorilla."

Got it, etc. …

What I found was that there are a few contributing factors to how well a person did on actually identifying MM. A huge factor was the order in which the images were shown – a variable I don't believe any other researchers considered. My experience showed that, generally, the first large, non-furry animal the locals didn't recognize is called MM. A rhino, elephant, or hippo would receive a few votes for MM using this technique. If there is an area with a lot of hippos but no rhinos, rhinos are called MM *if* the picture of the rhino is shown before the picture of the sauropod. If the picture of the sauropod is shown first, that invariably gets the vote. Hippos, elephants, even crocodiles can all be MM depending on whether the locals have ever really seen one of those animals, and if the image of that animal is shown before or after the image of the sauropod. I didn't mix in other dinosaurs, but I believe doing that could go a long way to explaining the Jurassic Park scenario and name confusion.

Furry or small animals were generally given a guess. "Leopard?" – close, jaguar; or "Pangolin?" – nope, armadillo, but that makes sense. Any animals that looked similar to ones they knew were guessed at: "Crocodile" – nope, it's a Komodo dragon, but I see why you'd think that. The occasional "I've never seen that animal" was thrown in, but it was generally for ones that looked really unusual and very distinct from those the tribes were familiar with, like a grizzly bear. This showed that the villagers were willing to guess and make assumptions, but only with animals similar to those they had seen or had heard about. They had seen crocodiles, and a Komodo dragon reminded them enough of a crocodile to think it might be one. If they had never seen a hippo, when shown a picture of one some would say, "Rhino?", while others would say, "It's in the water, it has huge teeth, is it a hippo?" This showed me they were naming the animal based on descriptions they had heard and extrapolations based on the surroundings of the pictures – it's in the water, hippos live in water, I've never seen a hippo, but this looks like how people describe it.

Another factor is "group think". Again, in my experience, you are rarely ever alone with one person from the village. As a Westerner, you are an oddity, a big deal in village life. There are people around you all the time, interested in everything you do. If you start showing one person a picture, within seconds there will be a crowd, and group think quickly takes over.

Often, there would be 30-45 seconds of discussion before they would give an answer about an image. They would argue a little, look to each other for support or other ideas, and present their collective reasoning: "This image... is... an elephant?", followed by a group smile meaning, "Did I get it right?" The guides and translators would pick up bits and pieces, but often it was rapid-fire conversation from five or six people in multiple languages and a full translation was too difficult. They would tell me it went something like:

"That looks like the animal Frank saw."

"No, Frank is crazy, he saw a hippo and everyone knows it."

"That animal *is* a hippo, I think."

"You've never seen a hippo!"

"Look at the skin, that's a rhino."

"That's not a rhino or a hippo, that's an elephant. Look at its legs."

"Oh yeah, I see it, yeah, that's an elephant."

Or, more tellingly:

"I think that's an elephant."

"No, look at its neck."

"That's a neck? I thought it was the elephant's nose."

"Look at those spikes. The only animal with spikes is MM."

"Maybe it's an elephant with spikes?"

"No! There are no elephants with spikes! That's MM, I'm sure."

Group think played into most of the responses. Unless the animal was very common, the tribe members wouldn't answer right away, and there would be some debate about its identity. We did call attention to this in the episode of *Beast Hunter* and made sure you can hear it going on when the pictures are shown. Again, I have to say how impressed I was with not just Nat Geo's support for but their insistence that we show the reality of what we found – that is truly rare in TV, and it was admirable. If it had been a different production company or a different channel, I know I would have been asked to say things I didn't believe, or at the very least sugarcoat or obfuscate the reality of what we were finding.

Another factor we didn't take into account, but I feel played a significant role in the process of ID'ing photos, was the angle or view of the animal in the photo. There was so much debate about most photos and we were using very clear, forward or side-facing, full-view animal pictures and drawings where the animal was seen in its classic environment. I would guess there would have been even more debate and incorrect responses if we only showed a portion of the animal, removed the background, or placed it in an unusual but not out of the question setting. This would more closely mimic the vast majority of MM sightings, where just a small portion of the animal was glimpsed briefly under less-than-ideal conditions. I wonder what the results would be if we just showed them a picture of an elephant's back leg with the foot submerged in water. Or a crocodile's back as it leaps out of the water, or a full-body leaping crocodile from a great distance, its body almost entirely out of the water with its head perpendicular to the surface of the water. Or a hippo's open mouth with splashing water all around it. Or a rhino from the back as it leans down to the water to drink. After hearing the translations of the conversations trying to identify the forward-facing, clear-as-day images of known animals and sometimes still getting them wrong, I'd have to imagine that the shots I've proposed above would flummox many of the people and lead to some interesting responses.

There are some animals that *really* look like a sauropod, especially when parts of their body are hidden. If you look at an elephant swimming, with its trunk raised as they are known to do, the head absolutely looks like an old-fashioned drawing of a brontosaurus' back with the trunk sticking up like a long neck with a small head on the end. The end of the trunk could even look like two eyes. Distance and size are incredibly hard to judge on the water, even for folks who are on the water all the time, as demonstrated in numerous scientifically-controlled experiments using objects of known sizes placed known distances from the viewer. That elephant head could look like a huge sauropod in the distance, especially at dusk, night, or in the rain. A long python hanging from a branch into the water could at a glance look like a long-necked animal in the water eating the leaves of the tree. When a crocodile jumps out of water its body can look like a long neck with a fearsome set of jaws. Many accounts of MM that we heard described a "head like a crocodile". Crocs don't jump that often – maybe it *was* a crocodile jumping out of the water. Elephants don't swim that often, and rhinos and hippos are virtually unknown in the regions where MM is spotted – their backs look a lot like an old drawing of a sauropod. Their prints, as they go to water to drink, look *exactly* like descriptions of MM prints. Is it more likely that people who I've seen misidentify elephants, rhinos, hippos, and crocs when shown perfect, full-body, head-on images may have occasionally mistaken one of these animals for MM, when all they caught was a glimpse of it, under less-than-ideal conditions, in a place where they wouldn't expect to see the animals but do expect to see MM? Or is it more likely they saw a living dinosaur, looking and behaving in a way that we used to think dinosaurs looked and behaved, but now know that no dinosaur ever looked or behaved? Meaning – MM is described as a dinosaur in as much as folks in the early 20th century knew about dinosaurs. (I'll explore this more in a bit.)

The people in the tribes are generally portrayed as possessing nearly superhuman powers of perception and animal-identification abilities, which I actually found to be true. I witnessed it firsthand on our hunt and numerous excursions into the forest. However, I found the ability did not extend beyond the animals they always encountered and depended on for their survival. The various tribes knew everything about bush pigs, local primate species, and other animals they would frequently hunt, but not nearly as much about animals which no longer lived in their territories, even being frequently unable to identify ideal photos of them. They knew of hippos, but hadn't seen them. Some knew elephants, but many noted that "everything I know about elephants I learned from my grandfather," because elephants had been hunted to near extinction from the regions these tribes lived in. Many couldn't answer questions such as "Can elephants swim?", and hotly debated their responses. Many bragged about killing crocodiles, but when pressed for details it turned out they had killed various monitor lizard species, which were seen frequently enough to be known, but not well. Also, a lot of species had different names even among individuals in the tribes:

"Oh, you call that a crocodile? I call that a lizard!"

"No, no, a lizard has longer legs and no ridges on its back."

"Yeah, the ones that live down by the bend in the river?"

"Yes, those are lizards, this is a crocodile."

"Wow, I always thought they were crocodiles down at the bend!"

"You're both wrong, those are caiman. Caiman are small, crocodiles are big."

"I thought caiman were the big ones!"

The name was less important than, "You don't want to get bitten by it." This was true of crocodiles and monitor lizards, so it didn't really matter what someone called it. Caiman don't live in Africa, but this name has become locally associated with a small crocodile. There are harmless millipedes around the village in all of the leaf litter – unless you bite them, then they secrete cyanide, but for all intents and purposes harmless. There are also very dangerous centipedes, a bite from which would send you to the nearest hospital which might be over a day's walk away. It would knock you on your ass for a couple days of intense pain. The villagers made no distinction between the two. They called them the same name (despite looking and moving very differently) and treated them the same – kill them on sight. I saw elders teaching their children how dangerous the millipedes were and how important it was to cut them into three pieces with their machete. They would do the same with snakes. All snakes were considered venomous, extremely dangerous, and would be killed on sight. I was catching millipedes one day and the tribe saw me and started telling me how brave I was. I let one crawl on my face and tried to explain the differences between the millipede crawling on me and the centipede at my feet. They were not having it. The children ran away screaming, "THE WHITE MAN IS CRAZY!", and the parents all looked at me like I had lost my mind.

The last thing I will mention about the tribes' identifying photos of MM is that which is also most likely to make true believers the angriest. These tribes are not well off. They are, in fact, very poor. They are often discriminated against, occasionally enslaved, forced out of their ancestral lands by logging and other outside influences, and generally not treated very well or given many opportunities to better their situations. They struggle to adapt to a new world that is not very kind to them. Expeditions to find MM have been going on since the 1920s, and these tribes are wise to them. Just as they broke out the grass skirts and shell jewelry when the cameras came out, they whip out well-rehearsed MM stories on demand, including everything you hope to hear. Don't get me wrong, they don't have crews lined up coming to visit their village – each tribe probably gets one MM expedition every four years – but the gifts brought to them by these crews are substantial. Generators, food, clothes, supplies, children's books and toys, water containers, etc. It was sad, but even our trash was prized by the tribes. They saved everything we discarded and reused all of it. They know the type of stories that keep people coming back and were happy to share them.

I don't want to ruin anyone's reputation with this book, but I got the distinct impression that many of the eye witnesses had been prepped before speaking with us. Some couldn't answer questions that deviated from the very apparently rehearsed version of their story, such as, "What season was your sighting in?" or "Did the creature make any noise?" On more than one occasion, Barny, who spoke French, heard folks who seemed more keen to keep the stories flowing, feeding other "witnesses" lines in a mix of French and Baka. When this would happen, we would stop the interview and ask, "What are you telling them?"

They would reply: "No, not telling them anything, just making sure they understand the question." In reality, Barny could hear them saying things like: "Tell them it was at night, and you saw the animal's head clearly, and it was small but had flat teeth," or "They think you're talking about a crocodile, you have to tell them that it wasn't a crocodile. Tell them the animal had a long neck and a small head and it stood tall on four legs, with a huge tail. Tell them the tail crashed into the water and made a wave that rocked your canoe." After the third time this happened we asked to do all interviews with only one person at a time and many of the stories we heard became far less detailed and much shorter. We edited all of these clearly rehearsed tales from the episode, but I'm afraid that it's possible that even the ones that made it in may have been tainted by the desire to bring more outsiders to the region.

"These massive sauropod-like animals aren't seen very often because the area is extremely remote. Also, they are seasonal, going into underground caves to hibernate during the hottest, driest months when the area is most accessible to outsiders and the most people are around. People have found tubes leading to these caves and have even found entrance ways large enough for a dinosaur to get in and out of."

I'll dispel this in two parts. First the isolation. The area is isolated, is hard to get to, and is very tough terrain – on land. By water? Not as tough. We saw a number of logging boats and heard logging equipment almost every day we were there. In the "Danger Zone" we produced camera-trap photos of people walking by (in small bikini briefs). We observed many people carrying smartphones. We saw villages along the river, homesteads, and occasional missions. By Western standards, it is extremely remote and very difficult to access. By Congo standards? It's a little out there. It would be like the American equivalent of rural Wyoming, I'd say. Most Americans haven't been there, and those that have stayed in Jackson Hole or Cheyenne, or charted a fishing expedition, and while you can go weeks, maybe even months, without seeing another person in parts of it, you're also not surprised to find an empty Coke bottle around the bend. My guess is that, if there was a dinosaur, we'd have a picture of it, or it would have done some damage to the logging companies by now.

Another common argument for MM's existence is well documented and was something our crew was excited to explore. Namely, cave systems in the region where MM could spend the hot, dry months. We spoke with a number of local "experts" whom I will not name before the shoot and they confirmed the existence of the caves and what they called "breathing tubes" or "air vents" – small tunnels going from the surface to the cave systems. One specific expert informed us that these tubes were about one foot in diameter and were over a hundred feet long. He said that most were unexplored, but the few that he'd been able to really investigate opened into a massive underground cave system. His theory was that this cave system was accessible underwater, and these small tunnels allowed for air exchange with the surface. These caves would be an ideal location for a huge animal to hide and "hibernate" during the warmest and driest seasons. This seemed to fit well with historical sightings of the animal, which occurred primarily when the river was highest, during the rainy season. The existence of these caves, the possibility to explore them using remote operated vehicles, and the statement from him that a large entrance had been uncovered by the unusually shallow conditions in the river led us to conclude that the end of the dry season was the best time for our expedition – and, that we should hire this individual to lead us. His name doesn't appear anywhere associated with the show and I'm not in the habit of ruining people's reputations – so I won't mention it here either – we'll call him Thomas.

I suspected something was fishy when no one in the tribe had ever heard of any cave or "breathing tubes" in the area. Thomas insisted they were real, but seemed very hesitant to bring us to them. He kept saying that, "They really need some more investigating." We told him that was exactly why we were there, to investigate, as we had spoken about on the phone. Thomas said we should first check out the misleadingly named "Danger Zone". As documented in the preceding chapter by the same name, the only danger in the "Danger Zone" was getting Kenny Loggins stuck in your head for days at a time. It became apparent after two days on the water that Thomas had no intention of showing us these breathing tubes or the caves. Barny and Laura finally insisted, saying they had discussed it at length, he had agreed to it in our contract, we had brought special gear to explore them, and his knowledge of their location was the primary reason for hiring him.

We had rigged a miniature remote-controlled off-road vehicle with a camera and lights and planned to send it down the tubes while we monitored the feed in real time. We also had ropes and gear to spelunk and the previously detailed sonar. None of this equipment proved necessary as none of the features described by Thomas exist. At least not where we were (I'll come back to that).

Let's get a little science out of the way first then go into what we actually found. I'll accept that Thomas used the term "hibernation" incorrectly and meant "aestivation" – I'm not going to argue semantics. Animals go into a state of dormancy to escape extreme conditions – sure, okay. My question is why would *this* animal need to develop this extreme survival strategy? It doesn't make sense. There isn't an environmental driver. I'm jumping ahead of myself with the "MM is based entirely on outdated ideas of dinosaur biology, physiology, and behavior," but let's look at why any vertebrate aestivates. The primary driving factor is lack of water, secondary is heat. Lungfish, frogs, toads, salamanders, crocs – all aestivate somewhere cooler and more humid than the ambient conditions of their normal environment. If you look at the areas where MM is supposed to live, there is plenty of water, even in the dry season. It's extremely humid year round, and temperatures don't fluctuate that much from season to season. I also won't go into massive explanations about endo vs. ectotherms, and the jury is certainly out on which camp, if either, sauropods fit with, but we do know they were not biologically "lizards" as previously thought, and we don't see any birds aestivate, even in areas where aestivation would be a good evolutionary strategy. We also know that sauropods couldn't swim, and would not be able to fully submerge their body to enter underwater caves due to air sacs and other bone structures.

So we can rule out the drivers of water and heat as a reason for aestivation and the underwater caves as a place to aestivate, and what are we left with? Food as a driver, and a lungfish-like mucus cocoon, maybe? I can tell you, there is plenty of food for a large herbivore. I saw fruit trees, figs, flowering plants, lots of leafy greens, nuts – just about every conceivable vegetarian option. It was kind of a vegetarian smorgasbord, actually. Rainforests are well known to be in "continuous bloom" – there really isn't a time when there isn't something to eat.

I'll get to the mucus cocoon in a little while. How about a little Earth science/physical geography first? That sounds fun, right? Question – what substrates are caves formed in? Answer – rocky ones, of gypsum, limestone, marble and the like. Not in clay riverbeds. The areas where MM is sighted do not have limestone, marble, or gypsum – they have clay. This was the first thing Barny, James, Duncan, Laura, and I noticed when we got to the water. We saw areas clearly worn down over the years by the river, and each layer of soil was just that – soil. There was no sandstone, no stone at all in fact. We asked the locals, "If you dig do you ever hit rock?"

The reply was, "No, this is good soil and clay forever." We, of course, did see rocks on the surface in some spots, but there was no "bedrock", as would be needed to form caves. Nor was there limestone or sandstone, as described by Thomas.

When Thomas finally, reluctantly, agreed to take us to the entrance of the cave (which had been exposed by the unusually low water levels) and the breathing tubes, we were relieved. At least we could explore them for ourselves. Even if the tubes didn't lead to a cave system, they might lead to a monitor lizard, or the larger "cave" might hide a large snake. The first time he pointed them out, we collectively groaned. "These aren't tunnels, breathing tubes, or air vents, Thomas. Those are clearly just little indents in the riverbanks and tubes that insects or rodents have dug out," said a frustrated Barny.

"Well, there are better ones. I'm just saying that is what they look like," said a visibly embarrassed Thomas.

"Okay, well, let's skip them for now and go to the cave entrance, please," was all Barny could muster. About an hour later we arrived at a bend in the river with a pretty visible mudslide that looked a few months old.

"This was a cave entrance that was covered up by a mudslide during the rainy season."

"Thomas, it doesn't look like a cave was here, and the bank is only 10 feet tall anyway. Even if the cave entrance took up the entire bank it would be a stretch to say this was big enough for a dinosaur to get into."

"No, no, it was underwater also."

The locals confirmed there used to be a small indent in the riverbank here, maybe four feet high, but there was no consensus on how deep it was – some said just a couple feet, others "pretty deep".

"Okay, Thomas, please take us to the cave entrance that is still open."

When we arrived, there was another collective groan.

"Oh, come *on*," said Laura.

Thomas, ashamed: "I said we needed to explore it more."

"There is absolutely nothing to explore! That's a small dent in the riverbank."

It was maybe four feet wide and three feet high. We didn't even need to break out our flashlights to see the back of it because it was only about two feet deep. It looked like a spot where a chunk of bank had fallen into the water. Nothing unusual at all.

"Should we even check out the 'air vents'?" Barny asked, annoyed.

We did, and they were as expected. There were tiny ones, no more than an inch in diameter that were clearly tunnels made by insects – we even saw some insects using them. Others were clearly rodent holes, snake holes, etc. – none large enough for the ROV to get down. We finally found one that appeared to be deep and wide enough, geared up the ROV, ran some tests, started recording, and sent it in. Within about 15 seconds it hit the back wall. It was maybe eight feet deep. We repeated this at five or six holes, all with the same result. None were more than 10 feet deep, none contained animals, and none led to underground, partially-submerged caves.

Now let's step away from caves and make a huge allowance for MM. Let's say it's completely unique amongst large animals (and all non-amphibious or aquatic animals) and employs a lungfish-like mucus cocoon, aestivating in the mud and clay during the dry season. First, I would have so many biological questions for how such a large-bodied animal would do this – the actual act of burying its 20-30 footlong self, complete with massive giraffe-like neck and tail, in mud without dying from exertion or collapsing its lungs with the pressure of the mud/ clay on its ribcage. Also, consider the lack of its ability to carry out a million biological processes like secreting the mucus sac, osmoregulation, and thermoregulation. And even assuming it could overcome all of that, the question of "why" remains. Why does the animal *need* to aestivate? What is the driver? Is the driver also unique in all of science?

Our answer has to be that it doesn't – this animal, if it exists, doesn't aestivate in caves or mucus sacs. Mostly because there are no caves, breathing tubes, or air vents, but also because there is no evidence that any animal even remotely like MM in size or possible classification has ever developed an adaptation like a lungfish's cocoon, or had reason to do so. There is no selective pressure from food sources, heat, humidity, or predation. You know, maybe I spoke too soon when I said, "The existence of MM wouldn't disprove evolution." I guess an animal with an adaptation that extreme – which uses a massive amount of energy and requires truly remarkable modifications to every aspect of its physiology yet provides absolutely no benefit to its continued survival other than making it conveniently "disappear" during the season when the most outsiders would be in an area – might go some distance towards showing intelligent design, if not full-on divine creation.

All of MM's traits and behaviors are based on outdated ideas of dinosaur biology, physiology, and behavior.
Admit it – when you think sauropod, you think of that brontosaurus picture in that book about dinosaurs that you had as a kid, don't you? It had grey-green, reptilian skin, was submerged up to its massive belly in a swamp, and was munching on some seaweed, wasn't it? There was probably even a sweet pterodactyl screeching overhead and a T-Rex lurking menacingly on the shore. Dinosaurs were awesome, weren't they? Too bad we were all completely wrong about them. Even their name "terrible lizards" is wrong. How bummed were you when you found out that velociraptors, the thinking, doorknob-turning menaces from *Jurassic Park*, were covered in feathers and would look like "kind of strange birds" if we saw them alive? Or that T-Rex's closest living relative was a chicken? (I *know* that's not actually true — the chicken bit — but I can picture my friend Darren cringing as he reads this — and it is essentially as true as saying a T-Rex's closest living relative is any other modern bird species — chicken is just so much more fun to say than Eagle). Anyway, like good scientists, we need to look at the latest evidence, analyze it and determine its veracity, and accept that dinosaurs didn't look nearly as badass as we thought. And they didn't behave, eat, or even move the way we thought they did. Interestingly – like your grandfather who still calls jeans "dungarees" and refers to certain groups of people as ... never mind that — MM appears to be stuck in the past. Amazingly, MM looks, behaves, eats, and moves just like we thought sauropods did in the early 1900s, when stories of MM

caught the nation's attention, but our hypotheses, like your grandfather's vocabulary, were wrong.

Sauropods didn't live in swamps, or stand in water up to their bellies. The most current research suggests that they had bird-like "hollow bones" and air sacs throughout their vertebrae, making them extremely buoyant. They wouldn't have been able to submerge their bodies to enter an underwater cave, or pop up near an unsuspecting fisherman. They couldn't walk in the water with just their neck out (as many eyewitness accounts suggest) or swim – a swimming sauropod would have been very unstable. They couldn't eat the plants on the side of the river without being on the side of the river themselves.

Sauropods lived entirely on land and moved in great herds covering significant distances. It is true that a very large group of gorillas (as many as 125,000 according to some estimates) were discovered in 2008 in the Congo, rightfully raising the question of "What else is out there that we don't know about?", but a herd of the largest land animals on Earth migrating great distances across lands being hit by illegal loggers seems like a stretch. MM, on the other hand, is supposed to be a loner, and fiercely territorial. They are said to destroy anything that enters their territory, and to only disappear from the waterways when they "hibernate". MM is also supposed to be very aggressive, killing any hippos it encounters. Sauropods were likely more defensive than aggressive, and would not be in the water with a hippo.

A solitary, hibernating, aquatic animal in the inner swamps of the Congo could probably stay hidden, but a migratory pack of giant land animals? We would see signs – tracks, droppings, teeth. Sauropods are thought to have lost teeth rapidly; some estimates say one species would have replaced its entire set every 14 days. They would disrupt poaching and logging operations. They would *be* poached! There would be an illegal trade in their feet, teeth, horns, and penises. I can't see an animal like this staying hidden, even with a staggering statistic like the gorillas.

Much like the famous "Nessie Pose" for the alleged plesiosaur in Scotland, modern science has shown that dinosaurs "just don't do that". A plesiosaur couldn't hold her neck up like a swan above water, and MM couldn't pop up under a fisherman's canoe and smash it to pieces. In fact, a sauropod probably couldn't hold its head straight up high for very long, and would have probably kept it more horizontal to the ground. No sightings of MM I am aware of describe a horizontal neck posture.

The need for MM – breaker of canoes

My favorite part about investigating MM was my realization that it doesn't matter if the physical animal is real – what matters is that people believe it's real. It's an important and socially accepted myth which allows the society of some tribes to function in the way they need to function and explain certain terrible truths in a palatable way. Richard Dawkins describes humans as natural myth makers – he says we have evolved into storytellers and story believers. We need these stories, regardless of their legitimacy.

The Baka and Bayaka peoples are tough – they have to be. I didn't see too many old people or babies in their villages. I saw a lot of incredibly strong people between the ages of 13 and 45. Their society rewards skill, strength, intelligence, and fearlessness. As I've mentioned in previous chapters, they file their teeth to fine points in order to look like carnivores, use elaborate scarification and tattooing to appear more fearsome, and wear John Cena T-shirts.

I was laughed at when I suggested they might be mistaking MM for a crocodile, a monitor lizard, a hippo, a rhino, or an elephant. Interestingly, the explanation for the laughter was not, "We would never confuse those animals! We know this land and everything in it!", but "We aren't afraid of those animals! We have spears, arrows, and hatchets! We can't be afraid of a crocodile! We kill crocodiles, our grandparents ate elephants!

The only animal we are scared of is Mokele M'bembe." I heard this again and again.

If a young Baka man didn't want to go down to the river at night because he was worried about crocodiles, he would be called a coward. If the same man didn't want to go down to the river because he was worried about encountering MM, he would be considered practical and smart, a pragmatic thinker even. The best hunters and fisherman, even the chiefs, were afraid of MM. They revered it. If it was spotted somewhere, they would avoid that location for a while. MM is the boogeyman that keeps kids in their beds at night, but more than that, it's the "out" card from choosing between doing something potentially fatal or being called a coward and losing people's respect.

It is a terrible idea to go to the river at night. Crocodiles and hippos are hard enough to spot during the day, and frequently kill people at night. During the rainy season the rivers run very fast and the currents are really strong. As I've pointed out, most fishermen cannot swim and are on unstable sampans all day. If your culture insists that you be strong and brave and not afraid of such real dangers as these, you need a way to prevent all of your young men from being killed.

I don't think it's a coincidence that MM is "spotted" when the river is the fastest, most unpredictable, and deepest, or in the same areas that would be ideal locations for crocs and hippos – sandy or muddy banks, small islands, and stretches with ideal basking or herding locations. I also see that in order to maintain this necessary lie, all of the villagers must buy into it and talk about it as if it's real. If adults admit the boogeyman is fake, the story loses its ability to keep people safe. Think about M. Night Shyamalan's much-maligned film *The Village* (which I enjoyed). Everyone had to *believe* in those creatures to keep people in the village. If a rumor spread that the woods weren't full of porcupine men, people would leave and teenagers would get curious and dare each other into riskier behaviors. The threat had to be real, so once in a while (Spoiler Alert) homes had to be raided and people injured – not fatally, but enough to keep them from *real* dangers (the outside world in the case of the film, crocs, hippos, and deadly currents in West Africa). And people *do* disappear in these regions, even when avoiding MM.

It seemed that most people who have been "killed" by MM were well known, well liked, and highly regarded. Whether this was true before their death or simply posthumous eulogizing I can't say. They were the strongest hunters, the best fishermen, and the best boatmen – but MM was better.

"Let this serve as a lesson to all, even *JEREMY*. Jeremy – who we all knew and loved. Jeremy – who could steer his sampan through the toughest rapid. Jeremy – who killed that croc with a knife, remember? Even Jeremy could not defeat MM. Parts of Jeremy's canoe washed up on the shore this morning. He went out on the river last night to get some extra fishing in. We heard those terrible noises last night, yes? We all know he could handle the rapids, his eyes were the best at night, and his arms were the strongest to haul in even the largest fish. But MM, the smasher of canoes, was stronger."

This was a typical story told when a well-respected fisherman/ hunter disappeared. It could not have been the ever-changing river, with new sandbars, rocks, and other hazards. It couldn't be a croc, or an out-of-place hippo, rhino, or elephant – only MM could take out someone like Jeremy. Even spotting MM brought you a certain status. In a small village, word spreads fast, and the story is repeated over and over by the fire at night and while fishing during the day. Your name gets mentioned – you survived the encounter! Even if you weren't 100% positive of what you saw at the time, you are after the third or fourth telling. We all know this happens.

"Hey, Jim thinks he saw MM!"

Jim: "I said I'm not *sure* what I saw. It was really big, it splashed a lot, and it looked like its back was huge with a long neck, but it was really far away."

"That sounds just like MM! Remember when Bill saw it last year! That's just what he said! It was really big, with a long neck."

Jim: "Yeah, maybe, I dunno. It was really far away."

Two weeks later, more people have asked Jim to repeat the story, and that pretty girl, Maria, has been paying more attention to Jim. Jim, with a crowd gathered around him, says:

"It was HUGE, and came up right next to my boat! The body was the size of three elephants and the neck was massive. I didn't see the head because of the spray of water from the enormous splash that rocked my canoe (glances at Maria), but I stayed on it, even though it was tipping back and forth like this (makes rocking motion; Maria smiles). It roared so loud and splashed the water again! I hauled in my net and paddled as fast as I could. I got away from it before it could smash my canoe with its tail."

We all exaggerate when people are paying attention to us. Stories get distorted. Our imagination takes over and creates memories of things that didn't really happen. This is what a species of "natural storytellers" does. We, unlike other animals, learn not just from our own successes and failures, but from the successes and failures of other members of our species, and even from their lies. Jonnie Hughes' book *On the Origin of Tepees* goes into this concept even more for those who want to check it out, but the gist is – we tell stories; we learn from stories; and we need stories.

Final synopsis

So you're telling me there's a chance? YEAH!
– Lloyd Christmas

As a legend, I love Mokele M'bembe. It's one of the more

fascinating stories in cryptozoology because of how many "needs" the tale satisfies. It allows local peoples to avoid very dangerous activities without being looked at as cowardly; it provides a revenue source for tribes, who share everything including the gifts researchers bring them; it maintains a link with the past when huge, fierce animals did roam the regions, and the Aka Pygmy (Baka, Bayaka, and others) peoples clashed with them; and it represents the intensely wild nature of the land and waterways that these people depend on. It's an animal that commands respect and reverence, just like the extraordinary jungle and swamp surrounding them. It's a creature outside the influence of the modern world, which has not been kind to the tribes. I'm so glad that I had the privilege to go and explore the legend for myself. With that said, I believe it should lie firmly in the realm of legend.

In order to accept that MM is a living dinosaur, you need to make a lot of exceptions. You need to get *really* creative with statements that start with, "It could happen, theoretically, if...", followed by a very far-fetched theory setting MM apart from all known animals and going against what we know about dinosaur physiology. Sure, the platypus doesn't survive the cut from Occam's famous razor, but there are 60,000 weevil species for every platypus. If you called me up and said, "I've just found an animal," without knowing anything about said creature, I'd bet it's a weevil and not a platypus. In trying to explain the existence of MM, you find yourself making so many exceptions, so many excuses, so many absurd one-offs in the fields of animal behavior, physiology, biology, earth science, geology and others, that it makes it feel like you're reaching a little too far, and describing the ultimate platypus. I'm sorry to say this, but in my mind it's case closed – there is no surviving dinosaur in Equatorial West Africa.

For those who absolutely want to believe in a living dinosaur, I should say, it is possible that Thomas led us astray. He may have kept the caves, tunnels, breathing tubes, and "real" Danger Zone hidden from us. I don't think he did — I don't think they exist — but I can't rule out the possibility. It just seems like such a strange lie that was guaranteed to be shown as a lie, that's it's odd to have told it in the first place, so maybe he didn't feel we were the right ones to reveal the true location to; I'll never know. Also, I didn't go to the Lake Tele region of the Congo. This lake was made famous by a Japanese research team's footage of a perfect blobsquatch, in which some "see what they want to see". In my mind, it's a boat or possibly a swimming elephant, but others see a swimming sauropod, marking the first time in the history of the Earth that a sauropod swam across a lake. Lake Tele had been a focus of MM researchers until some local guides earned a reputation for bringing people there then bribing them for obscene amounts of money to guide them back, or even threatening their lives. The veracity of these stories can't be confirmed, but they are persistent enough to keep many production teams away – ours included. It's not worth the risk. It's also incredibly harsh terrain, surrounded for miles by nearly impenetrable swamps. I do have a friend, Brady Barr, who went there and said it was fantastic and indescribably isolated. He said there may be some unknown species there, but it isn't dissimilar from other areas of the surrounding countries, and there would be no environmental or biological reason for a large, completely distinct animal to live there. Maybe a new species of snake, lizard, even a primate – but not a completely new class of animals. Also, regarding "MM is based on outdated dinosaur biology" – sauropods didn't live in swamps, half-submerged in water, munching on algae, the way your children's book imagined them. MM is likely the misidentification of a known species combined with a compelling societal pressure to perpetuate it's mythos. There are no living dinosaurs (except birds), and that's truly unfortunate. Not cool, Science, not cool.

Acknowledgements

While I have dedicated this book to Harry and Laura Marshall, I truly could not have completed it without the help of many incredible people who I am so fortunate to have in my life. I'd like to take a few pages to thank each of them.

Anna – my phenomenal wife. She not only joins me on many adventures, but has put up with all of the insanity that comes with being a partner to a guy who does all of the stuff described in here.

Our kids, Luna Caulfield and Wallace Charles. The greatest aspect of my life is being a part of theirs.

My insane and wonderful family – Al, Mom, Sarah, and Nathan who have supported and encouraged me throughout my life. Mom, who learned more about alligator reproduction than she probably ever wanted to in her quest to support a budding young biologist and Al who took me camping and fishing despite having no interest in these activities himself, which I never knew until I was in my late twenties. Sorry about child welfare having to come to the house and watch you change diapers and question Sarah about possible neglect/abuse after I got salmonella from a lizard, then spread it to about a dozen friends, and cracked my head open sledding, and sliced my legs open sliding down a hill to catch a snake – hopefully this makes up for the embarrassment?

The entire current and past Icon family, particularly Harry and Laura Marshall. Harry and Laura are two of my favorite people on Earth. They are the people Anna and I want to be when we grow up. They are the smartest, nicest, funniest, and most caring and loving people you could hope to meet, and the greatest thing about doing TV has been having them enter our lives. We love them like family. In addition to Harry and Laura there's Andie Clare, Lucy Middleboe, Stephen McQuillan, Barny Revill, James Bickersteth, Alex Holden, Anna Gol, Ben Roy, Laura Coates, Sol Welch, Belinda Partridge, Abi Wrigley, Duncan Fairs, Robin Cox, Simon Reay, Brendan McGinty, and everyone else, who continue to be amazing forces of encouragement and support.

The Nat Geo team behind *Beast Hunter* – Janet Han Vissering, Steve Burns, Ashley Hoppin, Sydney Suissa, Russel Howard, Chris Albert, Geoff Daniels, Mike Mavretic, Dara Klatt, Steve Ashworth, Whit Higgins, and others. Thank you so much for your support and trust in allowing me to fulfill a lifelong dream, and letting Icon take the lead and make a series we are all really proud of.

The most amazing and supportive group of friends I could ask for – Adam Manning, Dom Pellegrino, Joe Viola, and Adrianna Wooden. Thank you for sticking by me and being there for me and my family through everything.

Thank you so much to the entire team at John Hunt Publishing, especially John Hunt, who saw the potential of the massive and messy manuscript I sent over, Dominic James, who assured all of my insecurities and answered all of my questions while reassuring me that it was all going to be okay, and the expert editing of Graham Clarke, who managed to pull these six books together and make them the cohesive series.

My very literary friends and family who served as the first reviewers of this book – Al Spain, Joe Viola, Dom Pellegrino, Richard Sugg, Sarah Franchi, Gene Campbell, Tim Fogarty, John Johnson, Zeb Schobernd, Sarahbeth Golden, and Luke Kirkland

– thank you for your insights and mocking. This book is much better because of you.

The folks at my day job who have supported my insane extracurricular activities – especially Bill O'Connor who gave me the opportunity to do this and assured me I'd still have a job when I returned.

Thanks to all of the incredible fixers, guides, and translators who kept us alive and safe, often risking your own lives in the process.

Thanks, finally, to the readers and fans of these shows! I hope you've enjoyed what you've seen and read! You can find all of my social media stuff at www.patspain.com. I try to answer questions and respond as best I can. Genuinely – thank you!

Continue the adventure with the Pat Spain On the Hunt Series

A Little Bigfoot: On the Hunt in Sumatra
Pat Spain lost a layer of skin, pulled leeches off his neither
regions and was violated by an Orangutan for this book
Paperback: 978-1-78904-605-2
ebook: 978-1-78904-606-9

200,000 Snakes: On the Hunt in Manitoba
Pat Spain got and lost his dream job, survived stage 3 cancer,
and laid down in a pit of 200,000 snakes for this book.
Paperback: 978-1-78904-648-9
ebook: 978-1-78904-649-6

A Living Dinosaur: On the Hunt in West Africa
Pat Spain was nearly thrown in a Cameroonian prison, learned
to use a long-drop toilet while a village of pygmy children
watched, and was deemed "too dirty to fly" for this book.
Paperback: 978-1-78904-656-4
ebook: 978-1-78904-657-1

A Bulletproof Ground Sloth: On the Hunt in Brazil
Pat Spain participated in the most extreme tribal ritual,
accidentally smuggled weapons, and almost lost his mind in the
Amazonian rainforest for this book.
Paperback: 978-1-78904-652-6
ebook: 978-1-78904-653-3

The Mongolian Death Worm: On the Hunt in the Gobi Desert
Pat Spain ingested toxic "foods", made a name for himself in
traditional Mongolian wrestling, and experienced the worst
bathroom on Earth for this book.
Paperback: 978-1-78904-650-2
ebook: 978-1-78904-651-9

Sea Serpents: On the Hunt in British Columbia
Pat Spain went to the bottom of the ocean, triggered a bunch of
very angry fisherman, and attempted to recreate an iconic scene
from Apocalypse Now for this book.
Paperback: 978-1-78904-654-0
ebook: 978-1-78904-655-7

**6TH
BOOKS**

ALL THINGS PARANORMAL

Investigations, explanations and deliberations on the paranormal, supernatural, explainable or unexplainable. 6th Books seeks to give answers while nourishing the soul: whether making use of the scientific model or anecdotal and fun, but always beautifully written.
Titles cover everything within parapsychology: how to, lifestyles, alternative medicine, beliefs, myths and theories.
If you have enjoyed this book, why not tell other readers by posting a review on your preferred book site?

Recent bestsellers from 6th Books are:

The Afterlife Unveiled
What the Dead Are Telling us About Their World!
Stafford Betty
What happens after we die? Spirits speaking through mediums know, and they want us to know. This book unveils their world...
Paperback: 978-1-84694-496-3 ebook: 978-1-84694-926-5

Spirit Release
Sue Allen
A guide to psychic attack, curses, witchcraft, spirit attachment, possession, soul retrieval, haunting, deliverance, exorcism and more, as taught at the College of Psychic Studies.
Paperback: 978-1-84694-033-0 ebook: 978-1-84694-651-6

I'm Still With You
True Stories of Healing Grief Through Spirit Communication
Carole J. Obley
A series of after-death spirit communications which uplift, comfort
and heal, and show how love helps us grieve.
Paperback: 978-1-84694-107-8 ebook: 978-1-84694-639-4

Less Incomplete
A Guide to Experiencing the Human Condition Beyond the
Physical Body
Sandie Gustus
Based on 40 years of scientific research, this book is a dynamic
guide to understanding life beyond the physical body.
Paperback: 978-1-84694-351-5 ebook: 978-1-84694-892-3

Advanced Psychic Development
Becky Walsh
Learn how to practise as a professional, contemporary spiritual
medium.
Paperback: 978-1-84694-062-0 ebook: 978-1-78099-941-8

Astral Projection Made Easy
and overcoming the fear of death
Stephanie June Sorrell
From the popular Made Easy series, *Astral Projection Made Easy*
helps to eliminate the fear of death, through discussion of life
beyond the physical body.
Paperback: 978-1-84694-611-0 ebook: 978-1-78099-225-9

The Miracle Workers Handbook
Seven Levels of Power and Manifestation of the Virgin Mary
Sherrie Dillard
Learn how to invoke the Virgin Mary's presence, communicate
with her, receive her grace and miracles and become a miracle
worker.
Paperback: 978-1-84694-920-3 ebook: 978-1-84694-921-0

Divine Guidance
The Answers You Need to Make Miracles
Stephanie J. King
Ask any question and the answer will be presented, like a direct
line to higher realms... *Divine Guidance* helps you to regain
control over your own journey through life.
Paperback: 978-1-78099-794-0 ebook: 978-1-78099-793-3

The End of Death
How Near-Death Experiences Prove the Afterlife
Admir Serrano
A compelling examination of the phenomena of Near-Death
Experiences.
Paperback: 978-1-78279-233-8 ebook: 978-1-78279-232-1

Where After
Mariel Forde Clarke
A journey that will compel readers to view life after death in a
completely different way.
Paperback: 978-1-78904-617-5 ebook: 978-1-78904-618-2

Harvest: The True Story of Alien Abduction
G L Davies

G. L. Davies's most terrifying investigation yet reveals one woman's terrifying ordeal of alien visitation, nightmarish visions and a prophecy of destruction on a scale never before seen in Pembrokeshire's peaceful history.

Paperback: 978-1-78904-385-3 ebook: 978-1-78904-386-0

The Scars of Eden
Paul Wallis

How do we distinguish between our ancestors' ideas of God and close encounters of an extra-terrestrial kind?

Paperback: 978-1-78904-852-0 ebook: 978-1-78904-853-7

Readers of ebooks can buy or view any of these bestsellers by clicking on the live link in the title. Most titles are published in paperback and as an ebook. Paperbacks are available in traditional bookshops. Both print and ebook formats are available online.

Find more titles and sign up to our readers' newsletter at http://www.johnhuntpublishing.com/mind-body-spirit.

Follow us on Facebook at https://www.facebook.com/OBooks and Twitter at https://twitter.com/obooks.